Advanced and Struggling Students

Advanced and Struggling Students
An Insider's Guide for Parents and Teachers to Support Exceptional Youngsters

Parry Graham

ROWMAN & LITTLEFIELD
Lanham • Boulder • New York • London

Published by Rowman & Littlefield
An imprint of The Rowman & Littlefield Publishing Group, Inc.
4501 Forbes Boulevard, Suite 200, Lanham, Maryland 20706
www.rowman.com

86-90 Paul Street, London EC2A 4NE

Copyright © 2023 by Parry Graham

All rights reserved. No part of this book may be reproduced in any form or by any electronic or mechanical means, including information storage and retrieval systems, without written permission from the publisher, except by a reviewer who may quote passages in a review.

British Library Cataloguing in Publication Information Available

Library of Congress Cataloging-in-Publication Data
Names: Graham, Parry, author.
Title: Advanced and struggling students : an insider's guide for parents and teachers to support exceptional youngsters / Parry Graham.
Description: Lanham, Maryland : Rowman & Littlefield, [2023] | Includes bibliographical references. | Summary: "Based on the author's over twenty-five years in public education, Advanced and Struggling Students is a collection of insider information to help parents navigate the school system. Focusing specifically on the needs of struggling and high-achieving students, this book is a roadmap to help parents get the best for their child"-- Provided by publisher.
Identifiers: LCCN 2022047499 (print) | LCCN 2022047500 (ebook) | ISBN 9781475867176 (Cloth) | ISBN 9781475867183 (Paperback) | ISBN 9781475867190 (epub)
Subjects: LCSH: Public schools--United States. | Underachievers--Education--United States. | Gifted children--Education--United States. | Education--Parent participation--United States. | Parent-teacher relationships--United States.
Classification: LCC LA217.2 .G727 2022 (print) | LCC LA217.2 (ebook) | DDC 371.9--dc23/eng/20221207
LC record available at https://lccn.loc.gov/2022047499
LC ebook record available at https://lccn.loc.gov/2022047500

For Bryan—Mom would be proud that we both ended up in education, no matter what path we walked to get there.

Contents

Acknowledgments ix

Introduction xi

Section I: Struggling Students: Why, For Some Kids, School is an Uphill Marathon 1

CHAPTER 1: How Do I Know if My Child is Struggling? . . . 3

CHAPTER 2: I Think My Child is Struggling; How Do I Connect with the School to Get a Plan Started? 17

CHAPTER 3: How Do I Make Sure My Struggling Child is Getting the Support They Need? 25

CHAPTER 4: What Role Do Special Education and English as a Second Language Programs Play in Supporting Struggling Students? 41

CHAPTER 5: How Do Schools Identify and Support Struggling Students? 61

Section II: Advanced Students: Why the Most Successful Kids Often Get the Short End of the Stick 75

CHAPTER 6: What Does it Mean for a Child to be "Advanced"? 79

CHAPTER 7: How Do I Work With My Child's School to Figure Out if They Are "Advanced"? 89

CONTENTS

Chapter 8: What Should Schools Do to Support Advanced Students? 105

Chapter 9: How Do I Advocate for My Advanced Child? 125

About the Author 149

Acknowledgments

This book has benefited from the thoughts, conversations, and feedback of many people. My wife, Betsy, has spent years listening to me talk about the ideas in here, and countless hours reading through the many drafts. I owe a debt of gratitude to Eric Schwab, Ed Dehoratius, and Nicolas Rochoux for their encouragement, and especially to Dr. Alena Treat for her invaluable feedback and advice. I would like to thank the team at Rowman & Littlefield, in particular Tom Koerner, who helped to keep the project alive despite the pandemic. Un autre grand merci à mes amis Au Point Central à Lille.

And to all the educators and parents with whom I have had the privilege to work over the years—thank you. This book would not have been possible without your dedication and advocacy, and the lessons I learned from you.

Introduction

When I was young, my father was in the army and our family was stationed overseas. As a result, my kindergarten and first-grade years were spent in a school on a base in Germany. We came back to the States when I was seven, and our family never traveled out of the country again. But throughout my childhood I retained positive, if hazy, memories of our time abroad.

So, when I went to college, I resolved that I was going to get back to Germany. I finally made it when, during the summer after my sophomore year, I was able to participate in a work-study program in Berlin, where I would live with a German host family. I have a clear memory of arriving in Germany, exhausted from the flight, and meeting my host-father at the airport. One of the first things I did was try to ask him what time it was.

Despite having taken two years of German in college, however, what I said was completely wrong.

For the rest of the summer, I constantly struggled to understand and be understood. I would ask questions that I thought made sense, only to get blank stares in response. I would ask people to repeat themselves, only to be met with exasperation or condescension. And then, when I finally started to follow a conversation—when I started to feel a glimmer of success—the speaker would use a string of words that I'd never heard before, and I would be back to frustrated incomprehension.

Introduction

In my time in public education I have found that, for a lot of families, the experience of trying to navigate their child's school is a little like my experience in Germany. There are hazy memories from childhood, you have a sense that you *should* know how it works, but the language and the culture end up feeling confusing and intimidating.

In response, many parents either disengage to avoid feeling embarrassment, or they amp up their response to mask confusion with anger. But it doesn't have to be that way. Schools *should* be a place where parents feel welcomed. A place where rules and practices are translated into language that parents can understand and relate to. And a place where parents are provided the information they need to support and advocate for their children.

That's why I wrote this book. I have worked in public education for over twenty-five years at the elementary, middle, and high school levels, and I've worked with hundreds and hundreds of parents. I've seen the confusion and frustration on parents' faces when they just didn't understand what was happening with their child. When they wanted, more than anything else, to help their child be happy and successful, but they weren't able to translate what they thought their child needed into the language that schools spoke.

And this was especially true for the parents of students who struggled, and the parents of students who were high achievers.

My goal with this book is to teach you how to understand and be understood. To be your translator as you navigate the world of public education. One of the things I've learned in all my years in public schools is that a child's successful education rests on a partnership between the school and the home, but that partnership only works with effective, two-way communication.

I want to give you the language and the knowledge you need to be a productive partner with your child's school, and to be an effective advocate for your child's needs.

Introduction

ORGANIZATION OF THE BOOK

The book is organized into two parts: the first focuses on struggling students, and the second focuses on advanced students.

Each part contains multiple chapters, organized to provide you with the information you need to understand how schools work, and to effectively work with your child's school. There is no right or wrong way to read the book. You may want to jump directly to a chapter that addresses a challenge or question you're facing. Or you may want to start at the beginning and read until the end, looking for helpful information along the way.

Here is a quick description of each part, and the chapters that those parts contain. That will help you decide the best way *you* can use the book.

Struggling Students

The first part of the book is targeted at parents with a child who struggles in some way, providing specific advice on how to both support and advocate for a struggling student. The chapters in this part of the book address the following questions:

- *Chapter 1: How do you know if your child is struggling?* This chapter begins with a discussion of how schools define "struggling," and then provides concrete signs to look for and questions to ask your child's teacher(s).
- *Chapter 2: If you think your child is struggling, how do you connect with the school to get a plan started?* You will find a number of different scenarios in this chapter to help you think through your concerns, and to help you develop a plan to contact your child's school.
- *Chapter 3: How do you make sure your struggling child is getting the support they need?* Intervention plans are a key part of a school's approach to supporting struggling students. This chapter will introduce you to the elements of

INTRODUCTION

a successful intervention plan, and then shifts to talking about how you can support your child outside of school.

- *Chapter 4: What role do special education and English as a second language programs play in supporting struggling students?* For children with identified disabilities, or who are learning to speak English, there are special support systems in place in public schools. This chapter will provide you with a broad overview of those programs, while also sharing some specific information and advice.

- *Chapter 5: How do schools identify and support struggling students?* The final chapter of this section provides more technical information that is referred to elsewhere in the first part of the book. It looks at how schools typically identify struggling students, provides detail around the types of interventions that schools might have in place, and discusses the trade-offs that are important for parents to consider when their child receives interventions.

Advanced Students

The second half of the book is focused on parents who have students with advanced academic ability. The chapters in this part of the book address the following questions:

- *Chapter 6: What does it mean for a child to be advanced?* This chapter explains what it means to be an "advanced" student. You will be introduced to the types of evidence that might indicate advanced status, and learn about several factors that can complicate a determination that a student is advanced.

- *Chapter 7: How do you work with your child's school to figure out if they are advanced?* You will find seven scenarios in this chapter, each describing a common situation that parents might encounter as they work with a school to

Introduction

determine if a child might be advanced. The scenarios cover elementary, middle, and high school situations.

- *Chapter 8: What should schools do to support advanced students?* This chapter begins by talking about some foundational educational concepts that help explain schools' approaches to educating advanced students. It then shifts to looking at the right combinations of practices that you should hope to see at the elementary, middle, and high school levels to support advanced kids.

- *Chapter 9: How do I advocate for my advanced child?* The final chapter of the book covers three topics. The first is the general process for advocacy: who to talk to and how to talk to them. The next topic is the non-traditional advanced student, including students who are advanced in non-core subject areas, who have an identified disability, who possess social-emotional challenges, or who have weak executive functioning skills. The third part of the chapter provides advice on how to advocate for general programs or practices for advanced students.

Final Notes

Before you dive in, there are a couple final notes about the book. The first two are about language.

Throughout the book the terms "parent" and "parents" are used frequently, but those terms are meant very broadly. Children can be raised by a wide range of caregivers: biological parents, legal guardians, adopted parents, a grandparent, a foster parent, and so on. When the word "parent" is used, it means anyone operating in the role of a formal caregiver for a child.

The book also switches interchangeably between referring to male and female students. In some instances there may be generalized, gender-based patterns that are highlighted, but the rest of the time the intent is simply to try to be inclusive in the use of

INTRODUCTION

gender-specific pronouns. So, when the pronouns *he*, *she*, or *they* are used, the intent is not to draw attention to a specific gender.

Within the book you will find a variety of stories to provide concrete examples of more abstract ideas or advice. All of the stories in the book are drawn from actual situations that occurred, but in most cases enough details have been changed that the real-life people who formed the basis of the stories would not be able to recognize themselves. The intent is to provide an accurate look at what happens in schools, while also protecting people's privacy.

Finally, this is a book that is grounded in lived experiences. In various places there will be references to educational research, but the intent is not to give the reader a dissertation. Instead, the goal is for you to have an accurate, readable, experience-based guide to the realities of how public schools work.

Section I
Struggling Students
Why, For Some Kids, School is an Uphill Marathon

One of the iconic events that takes place every year in Massachusetts is the Boston Marathon. If you've ever run it, then you know that it can be a grueling experience, but the absolute toughest part of the race is something called Heartbreak Hill. It comes in the last half of the run and, while it may not be the longest or steepest hill around, it feels like an endless climb up a merciless slope.

For too many students, the public-school years feel like one long, unending Heartbreak Hill. These are students for whom school is difficult, students who struggle to be successful, and students whom schools struggle to support.

There are many possible reasons why a student might struggle in school—a lack of early reading skills or social-emotional challenges, just to name a few—and there are a variety of ways for schools to try to help struggling students. But for those kids whose schooling experience feels like an endless, uphill marathon, it is critically important for you, the parent or guardian, to be a knowledgeable and committed advocate. That's what the first half of this book is all about.

The first chapter will help you identify whether or not your child might be struggling. In the second and third chapters, you

Section I

will learn how to connect with your child's school to begin working on a support plan, and how to make sure your child is getting the help they need. The fourth chapter is a specialized chapter focusing on students who might qualify for special education or English language services. Finally, the fifth chapter provides technical information that is referred to elsewhere in the book, such as types of interventions and the trade-offs that can occur when interventions are put into place.

Chapter 1

How Do I Know if My Child is Struggling?

Every parent wants their child to do well in school: get good grades, make friends, develop a positive sense of self, and come home each day with a smile. When that doesn't happen—when a child instead brings home stories of struggle and frustration—it's hard to know what to do.

This chapter will help you figure out if your child's negative school experiences are just normal bumps in the road, or a true sign of distress. Every kid has good days and bad days, and there is value in sometimes allowing children to work through their own challenges. But when a child is truly struggling, it's important to take quick and appropriate action.

This chapter begins with a brief discussion about how schools define "struggling." As you will see, the definition that schools use is oftentimes not the same one that parents might. The remainder of the chapter provides concrete things for you to look for, and questions to ask your child's teacher(s), to help you determine if your child might be struggling.

What Does it Mean to be a Struggling Student?

It's not a simple thing for a parent to determine if their child is struggling. If your first child was a rock star student where

CHAPTER 1

school always came easy, then you might think your second child is "struggling" if things are tougher. If your child's peer group is filled with kids in Advanced Placement classes earning As, then you might think your B-average child is "struggling" because he's not in the same place as his friends.

Most likely, your child's school would not consider these situations to meet the definition of "struggling." To educators, the term doesn't mean "not doing as well as we would like or expect." Instead, a "struggling student" is typically one who is performing significantly below grade-level expectations.

Going back to the marathon analogy that started this section, the "finish line" in public education is graduation. In order to get there—in order to successfully complete the race—a student needs to demonstrate that they have mastered certain skills and knowledge along the way. Schools therefore expect that kids will meet specific milestones by the end of each year.

Now, you might be frustrated that your child doesn't seem to be able to run as fast or as far as you would like, but if your child is reaching those milestones by the time the school expects, then your child is demonstrating grade-level skills. She is "at grade level." If your child is beyond where the school expects by the end of a year, then she is "above grade level." But, if your child is not as far along as the school expects, then she is "below grade level."

A struggling student from a school's perspective is a student who is significantly below grade level, someone who should be passing the five-mile marker by the end of the year but is instead still stuck at mile three.

While schools are primarily focused on academic skills when making this determination, behavioral and social-emotional development also have milestones that schools will pay attention to. These can feel "squishier" and harder to objectively assess, but teachers and schools will likely flag students who seem to be struggling with their interpersonal skills or with following classroom and school rules.

The remainder of the chapter will focus on more concrete examples of what "struggling" can look like, with early elementary, later elementary, middle school, and high school examples. You will also find a number of questions that you can ask your child's teacher(s) to help you determine if your child might be struggling.

How Can You Tell if Your Child is a Struggling Student?

The warning signs of a struggling student tend to change as kids progress through the K-12 system. Here are concrete examples that can help you know if your child is struggling, broken out by different schooling levels.

Kindergarten through Second Grade

In early elementary, the most important academic skill to focus on is reading progress. If your child is not reading at grade-level, that is a warning sign to pay attention to (not necessarily a "the world is about to end" situation, but a warning sign nonetheless). Next is progress in math skills. And finally, the development of age-appropriate social skills and behaviors.

Now, how do you know whether your child is meeting grade-level expectations? The first answer is, talk to the teacher. There's nothing wrong with a bit of home-based diagnosis; for example, if your kindergarten child doesn't know all of his letters, can't count to 10 independently, or is completely unable to write any of the letters in his name, then he is likely starting kindergarten behind expectations.[1]

But teachers have a far better frame of reference than most parents, and they can distinguish between kids who might be a bit behind but will likely catch up, and kids who are truly struggling.

Elementary schools typically have teacher conferences scheduled multiple times over the course of the year. In addition, most teachers will be happy to schedule a teacher conference at your request at any time during the year. When meeting with your

CHAPTER 1

child's teacher to discuss their progress, there are a variety of questions to ask to help you determine if your child might be struggling:

- Are my child's reading skills at grade-level? If not, where are they? If they are below grade-level, what do you see as the possible causes?
- Are her math skills at grade-level? If not, where are they? If they are below grade-level, what do you see as the possible causes?
- When my child started the year, where were her academic skills relative to what you expect to see in an incoming student?
- Is my child demonstrating age-appropriate social skills and behaviors?

Some parents get very focused on the work that they see their child bring home. They worry that their child's handwriting looks atrocious, or they keep seeing a teacher highlight the same sorts of mistakes over and over. Rather than paying too much attention to comments on student work, however, it's more important to pay attention to the big picture feedback from your child's teacher, as opposed to comments on individual assignments.

One area that *is* important for you to pay attention to at home (in addition to asking for feedback from the teacher), is your child's social skills and behavior. Children who enter kindergarten with poor social skills—for example, they have significant difficulty cooperating with peers, they have a hard time ever understanding other children's feelings, or they are rarely able to resolve problems independently—are at significant risk of academic difficulty later on. In fact, effective social skills can be even better predictors of success in school than early academic behaviors.[2]

Now, most young children are going to struggle with peer interactions in some situations—the fact that your child took a toy away from another kid is not a reason to panic. But children who are significantly below grade-level expectations for social behavior are one type of "struggling" student. If you notice that your child seems to struggle in social situations relative to other kids, make sure to ask his teacher what she sees in the classroom.

Third Grade through Fifth Grade

By late elementary most children are beginning to master the mechanics of reading, and the focus turns toward a child's ability to understand grade-level texts. If your child is still struggling to sound out relatively simple words and has not developed an extensive list of sight-vocabulary (i.e., words that your child recognizes immediately without having to sound them out), those could be signs of academic struggle. Even if your child is doing okay with the mechanics of reading, an inability to understand what he is reading could be problematic.

At home, a good way to spot some reading difficulty is to have your child read to you on a regular basis. Make sure to pick some texts that are appropriate for his grade level (you can often get leveled readers from the teacher, and many booksellers and libraries indicate the reading level of children's texts). As your child reads, ask yourself:

- Does he struggle to pronounce relatively simple words?
- Does he have a hard time reading with expression (for example, making a question sound like a question, or a command sound like a command)?
- When you ask him to explain in his own words what is happening in the text, does he struggle to do so?

Chapter 1

In addition to what you see at home, make sure to get the teacher's opinion about your child's reading skills, either through a regularly-scheduled parent-teacher conference or through a conference that you request because of concerns. Some good questions to ask are:

- Has the teacher tested your child's reading level? If so, how does it compare to grade-level expectations?
- Is the teacher seeing your child make appropriate progress with reading (for example, maybe he started behind but is catching up, or maybe he started at grade-level but is falling behind)?
- Is your child regularly able to comprehend grade-level texts on a variety of topics (both fiction and non-fiction)?

Beyond reading ability, it is important to know if your child seems to be mastering skills and knowledge in other subject areas, such as social studies and science. These topics can also connect to reading—the more a child knows about a topic, the better able they are to read texts that cover that topic. If your child is struggling to learn information in other subjects, that could be an indicator of an underlying learning challenge. It could also presage difficulty in those subject areas when they get to middle school.

Math is another important area to pay attention to. By the end of elementary school, students are learning mathematical concepts that lay the foundation for more advanced work in middle school. Students who have incomplete mastery of these concepts will struggle to remain at grade-level with the more complex work that comes between sixth and eighth grade. Some questions to ask the teacher about your child's math progress include:

- Is my child making appropriate progress in automating some of the basic math skills (for example, memorizing

multiplication tables, or being able to do addition and subtraction in his head)?
- Does my child demonstrate grade-level understanding of different mathematical concepts (for example, what a fraction or a percentage represents)?
- Do you see areas in which my child is struggling that could impact his success in middle school math?

Just as it was important to keep an eye on social skills and behaviors in early elementary school, it is important to monitor the development of those skills in late elementary. Do remember that all kids can be squirrelly from time to time—just because your child wears you out on occasion doesn't mean that she has deficient social skills (although maybe deficient parent-pleasing skills). Some good questions for the teacher around social skills development are:

- Does my child demonstrate age-appropriate social behavior?
- Does my child appear to have friends at school? Does she seek out other students during unstructured social time (recess, lunch, etc.)?
- Is my child able to follow classroom rules effectively? Does she require frequent redirection from you?

One final point to mention. In late elementary, most public-school students will begin taking state-administered standardized tests, typically in at least reading and math. When you receive the results of those tests, your child's scores will likely be reported as a percentage. For example, if your child scores in the 55th percentile, then that means your child did better on the test than 55 percent of their same-grade peers taking the test state-wide.

CHAPTER 1

If you see your child repeatedly scoring poorly on state standardized tests, that could be an indication of academic struggle. It's important not to put too much stock in the results from any one year, but if your child is regularly scoring below the 25th percentile over multiple years, that could be a sign that your child has lower academic ability and is at risk of struggling academically.

Signs of a Struggling Middle School Student
The big sign of a struggling student in middle school is low grades. If your child is earning Ds and/or Fs in several classes, then your child is not achieving at grade-level expectations. Now, there could be a variety of reasons for this underachievement, but a pattern of low grades is the surest sign of a struggling student. (Important note: Some middle schools use what is called "standards-based reporting," as opposed to letter grades. With standards-based reporting, a pattern of below-standard or below-proficient academic achievement across multiple classes could be a sign of a struggling student.)

Nevertheless, grades aren't always the most accurate predictors of struggle, and they aren't the only signs to pay attention to. Here's a real-life example: A middle school in which basically every kid earns an A or a B in sixth grade, only to get pounded with much lower grades when they get to seventh grade. The reason for the disparity is that the teachers in the different grade levels have completely different grading philosophies: the sixth-grade teachers want to take it easy on the kids as they transition to middle school, while the seventh-grade teachers want to toughen the kids up after the "coddling" they received in the previous grade.

In this unfortunately true example, the kids are caught in the middle and the poor parents have no idea what to think: in sixth-grade, they assume their kids are doing just fine, only to panic and think those same kids are way behind just a year later.

So, while class grades are a good place to start, make sure you dig deeper by also focusing on key academic skills and social-emotional behaviors.

Middle School Academic Skills

Reading skills remain super important as students transition to middle school. It is tougher to accurately measure them than it was in elementary, but here are a couple signs that your child might be struggling to read at grade-level:

- Your child had a history of struggling with reading in elementary school.
- Your child takes a long time to read relatively short reading passages assigned for homework.
- When you have your child read a grade-level text out loud to you, she struggles with at least 1 out of every 10 words.
- When you ask your child to tell you about a grade-level text that she has read, she struggles to accurately summarize the important information and action.

When you meet with your child's teachers for parent-teacher conferences (either because the school scheduled them or because you requested a conference), there are a number of important questions to ask if you believe your child might be struggling:

- In English class, does my child appear to have grade-appropriate reading skills?
- In English class, is my child able to write with grade-level proficiency?
- In math class, does my child have the foundational skills and knowledge that she needs from elementary school and/or prior grades to master the curriculum?

CHAPTER 1

- In math class, do you see areas in which my child is struggling that could impact her success in high school math classes?
- In any class, does my child show evidence of being able to successfully read grade-level texts in your subject area?
- In any class, do you find that my child has the requisite background knowledge to understand new concepts in your subject area?
- In any class, when my child started the school year, did she show evidence of having grade-level skills?

By middle school, students should have taken a variety of standardized tests. As was true in late elementary, these standardized tests can provide insight into your child's academic progress. With the same proviso that one year with a low standardized test score probably doesn't mean much, a string of years with scores below the 25th percentile could indicate some real academic struggles. Conversely, reasonably high standardized test scores but low class grades might suggest a student with plenty of academic potential, but poor realization of that potential.

Middle School Social-Emotional Behavior

The final area to pay attention to is social-emotional behavior. Middle school students are known for being particularly moody (to a certain extent, they can't help that—their bodies and brains are going through huge hormonal changes), so it can be hard to distinguish real social-emotional challenges from the baseline craziness of early adolescence. But if you suspect that your child might be struggling in this area, here are some questions to ask your child's teachers or guidance counselor:

- Does my child behave in age-appropriate ways in class?

- Does my child appear to be able to form appropriate peer friendships?
- Compared to other students, does my child seem happy?
- Is my child able to successfully resolve conflicts with peers?
- Do you notice my child behaving in any unusual or abnormal ways, relative to peers?

Also within the social-emotional domain is school discipline. If your child regularly gets in trouble at school, especially if he is getting in trouble across multiple classes or has multiple referrals to school administration, this can be a sign of a social-emotional challenge that is worth addressing.

Signs of a Struggling High School Student
The signs of a struggling high school student are similar to those of a struggling middle school student, albeit with a few differences. Two of the big similarities are grades and standardized test scores. If your child has Ds and Fs across multiple classes, or if your child scores especially poorly on standardized tests (below the 25th percentile), those could be signs of struggle. The proviso, however, is that this doesn't mean low grades in high-level classes (Honors or Advanced Placement classes, for example). If a student with Ds and Fs in high-level courses is capable of earning reasonable grades in mid-level courses, then the student would not be considered to be "struggling."

One big difference between middle school and high school is the use of credits. In middle school, students typically move forward to the next grade level independent of the course grades that they received during the year (it is possible for middle school students to be retained and repeat a grade, but that is pretty rare). In order to graduate from high school, however, students do not just need to be in school for four years, they need to earn a specified number of credits. And in order to earn credits, students need to pass courses; failing a course means that a student gets no credit and may need to retake the course.

So, one measure of a struggling high school student is that she is behind in her credits. Students typically fall behind in earning credits because they have failed classes, but it can also be due to other reasons. For example, some high schools tie credits to attendance; in other words, if a student misses too many days of school, she can lose credits in her classes even if she earns a passing grade.

Attendance is therefore one of those additional things that high school parents need to watch out for. Especially when students become older and have greater responsibility for getting themselves to school (whether driving, catching a ride with a friend, walking, or riding public transportation), students can fall behind in their academic progress because they miss too much school. If your child has missed a significant amount of school for whatever reason—an ongoing health concern, a mental health challenge, skipping school—that could lead to academic struggles. As a rule of thumb, it is especially problematic for a student to miss more than 8 days in a quarter, 15 days in a semester, or 30 days in a year.

Overall, however, it is unusual for a high school student to suddenly develop academic difficulties. More commonly, a high school student who is struggling academically either has a history of academic difficulty or is dealing with a social-emotional challenge. Poor attendance is typically a symptom of a social-emotional challenge, but it is only one of the possible pitfalls that can catch otherwise academically-capable kids. Substance abuse, eating disorders, and emerging mental health challenges can all crop up in high school and cause a student to struggle. Some common signs of a social-emotional challenge at the high school level include:

- Poor attendance, as previously mentioned
- A drop in grades in multiple courses at a level at which your child has previously succeeded

- A pattern of disciplinary problems at school, where there were no prior issues in middle school
- Significantly uneven sleep patterns
- Abnormally high levels of irritability and defiance (beyond what one might normally expect from a teenager and beyond what you have seen in the past with your child)

If you see some warning signs or have concerns, the best person to reach out to is your child's guidance counselor. Schedule an appointment with him, and ask him to speak to your child's teachers and ask the following questions:

- Is my child achieving at his ability level in your class? If not, to what might you attribute his under-achievement?
- Does my child appear alert and focused in your class?
- Does my child behave appropriately in your class?
- Does my child have positive peer relationships with other students in your class?
- Has my child made any comments or behaved in ways that concern you?

Notes

1. There are plenty of helpful resources available on this subject if you're interested in learning more. One place to start is https://www.education.com/magazine/article/kindergarten-readiness-secrets.

2. Jones, D. E., Greenberg, M., and Crowley, M. (2015). Early Social-Emotional Functioning and Public Health: The Relationship Between Kindergarten Social Competence and Future Wellness. *American Journal of Public Health*, *105*(11), 2283–90. http://doi.org/10.2105/AJPH.2015.302630

https://www.ncbi.nlm.nih.gov/pmc/articles/PMC4605168/

CHAPTER 2

I Think My Child is Struggling; How Do I Connect with the School to Get a Plan Started?

In the previous chapter, the big question to answer was: "Is my child struggling?" If your answer to that question was "Yes," then it's important to connect with the school to begin putting a support plan together.

Figuring out your next steps, however, will depend on the nature of your concern. Is it less serious, or more serious? Is it just in one class, or across multiple classes? Is it primarily an academic concern, or are there social-emotional components?

This chapter provides a number of different scenarios to help you think through your concern, and to help you develop a plan to contact your child's school. Read through the scenarios to determine which one best matches your child's situation.

When you do reach out to the school, it's important to be as specific and evidence-based about your concern as possible. For example, a statement such as "It seems as if Robert is having a hard time" may not get you very far. A clear statement such as, "In the last two months, Robert's grades have dropped at least 10 points in three of his classes, and he seems to be fighting with me every night about doing his homework" is far more likely to light a fire.

Less Serious Academic Concern in One Subject Area or Course

An elementary school example of this situation might be a child who appears to be making slow reading progress, but is not struggling in a big way. A middle or high school example would be a child who receives a low quarterly grade on his report card in an individual course (for example, a low C or a D), but is not failing the course outright.

In these situations, the right person to contact is the classroom teacher. An email is the best way to make contact, with a brief but specific description of the concern (for example, "I am writing because my child seems to be having a difficult time in your class. Her last three quiz grades were all below 70, and this is out of character for her in this subject.").

Your goal is to set up a face-to-face meeting with the teacher to discuss your concerns and analysis of the situation, to hear the teacher's thoughts, and to reach agreement on what course of action will help. Beware an attempted email brush-off! The teacher may try to use email to develop a plan, or even to assure you that there is no need for one. Politely but firmly stick to your meeting request. A face-to-face meeting is much more likely to generate a productive outcome. A phone call could be an acceptable alternative, but face-to-face meetings are generally more effective.

More Serious Academic Concern in One Subject Area or Course

An elementary example of this situation might be a child who is really struggling (i.e., well below grade level expectations) with his reading or math progress. A middle or high school example would be a child who has a failing quarterly grade in an individual course. Typically, the right person to contact would be the classroom teacher; the exception would be if you have concerns about the effectiveness of the teacher.

If you believe the teacher may be part of the problem, then a guidance counselor, a subject specialist (for example, a reading or math specialist), a department chair (this would only apply at the high school or maybe the middle school levels), or even an assistant principal might be a good first contact. They may ask you to reach out to the classroom teacher first, which is a fine response and a reasonable thing for you to then do. But it doesn't hurt to get your concern about the teacher on someone else's radar.

Email is the best way to initiate this contact, and you should provide a pretty detailed description of your concern. Your goal is to set up a face-to-face meeting with the teacher to develop a plan to address the situation, which could potentially include formal interventions. As mentioned above, don't settle for an email brush-off—make sure you get a face-to-face meeting.

Low-level Academic Concern Across Multiple Subject Areas or Courses

In an elementary classroom, this might be a student who is somewhat behind in reading and math. A middle or high school example would be a student with low end-of-quarter grades (in the low C or D range) across several courses. At the elementary level, the best person to contact is the classroom teacher, with the goal of setting up a face-to-face meeting. The steps and process are similar to those described for a student with a less serious academic concern in one subject area.

At the middle or high school level, it's recommended that you send one e-mail to all of the teachers in whose classes your child is struggling. In the email, identify any common elements that exist across classes (for example, "It seems as if my child scored poorly on quizzes and tests across each class during the last quarter") while also listing situations particular to individual courses (for example, "In Science, he received failing grades on all three of his lab write-ups during the quarter"). Sending a joint email gives the teachers some insight into how your child is doing in other classes, which may prompt some insights or suggestions on their part. In terms of a next step, you could either look to meet with all of the teachers at the same time (which would make more sense in middle school) or to meet with the teachers individually (which would make more sense in high school).

In addition to contacting your child's teachers, you should also carbon copy your child's guidance counselor to make sure she is in the loop on your concerns. In fact, the guidance counselor may be in a position to meet with all of the teachers as a group, and then sit down with you separately to put together a plan of action.

More Serious Academic Concern across Multiple Subject Areas or Courses

For an elementary student, this would mean being well below grade level in both reading and math, and potentially in writing as well. For a middle or high school student, this would mean having failing quarterly grades on a report card in multiple subjects. As was the case with an elementary student with a serious academic concern in one subject area, the right person to contact would typically be the classroom teacher, unless you have concerns about the teacher's effectiveness. In that case, follow the advice above about other contact possibilities. And similar to the situations above, your goal is to schedule a face-to-face meeting with the classroom teacher.

In middle and high school, it's recommended that you send one email to all of the teachers in whose classes your child is struggling, describing concerns across classes and in individual classes. Definitely carbon copy your child's guidance counselor. Your goal is to set up a collective meeting with all of these teachers at the same time. Your child's guidance counselor should be able to help facilitate that meeting.

LOW-LEVEL BEHAVIORAL OR SOCIAL-EMOTIONAL CONCERN

In an elementary classroom, this might be a student who is having difficulty building relationships with peers, who regularly complains about not liking school, or who seems to get into minor amounts of trouble with the teacher on a weekly basis about following classroom rules.

For a middle or high school student, examples would include a child who seems to have difficulty forming friendships with peers, who is regularly unhappy at school, who has gotten in trouble multiple times within a couple weeks in one or more classes, who is experiencing changes in sleep patterns, who demonstrates an especially high level of irritability and defiance, or who is having poor attendance that is not easily explained by a medical circumstance.

At the elementary level, contact the classroom teacher via email with the goal of setting up a face-to-face meeting. Your email should contain enough detail and evidence to give the teacher a specific idea of your concerns and what leads to them. In middle or high school, a guidance counselor is probably the best first point of contact, unless the situation is specific to an individual class. For example, if your child has been assigned detention by the same teacher multiple times in the last several weeks, your best bet is to reach out to and meet with just that teacher. If the situation is not specific to an individual class, then set up a face-to-face meeting with your child's guidance counselor.

MORE SERIOUS BEHAVIORAL OR SOCIAL-EMOTIONAL CONCERN

At the elementary level, some examples might be a child who is having regular school refusal issues, who feels severely isolated at school, who does not appear to be able to relate to peers, or who regularly gets into trouble with the teacher for relatively significant behaviors (for example, physical aggression, destruction of school property, or threats toward other students).

At the middle school level, this could be regular school refusal, depression, substance abuse, a pattern of inappropriate online activity, an eating disorder, significant mood swings, or regularly getting into disciplinary trouble for relatively significant behaviors across multiple classes. High school examples could be similar to middle school, but might also include regular problems with attendance, significantly uneven sleep patterns, or more significant examples of substance abuse.

The first point of contact should be a guidance counselor but, depending on the situation, you may also want to contact a school administrator (probably an assistant principal). Your goal is a face-to-face meeting with the guidance counselor and/or administrator, who can then work with you to figure out whether or not teachers should be brought into the discussion. In your initial email to set up the meeting, provide enough information so that the recipient understands the general nature of your concerns (for example, that a string of disciplinary incidents has you worried about your child's progress), but you're advised against going into too much detail in the email. Because social-emotional and behavioral issues can be highly personal and private, it is best to share the details in a face-to-face meeting, rather than in an email.

One last point—in addition to reaching out to the school, you may want to look into professional support for your child. While schools can often provide a range of behavioral and social-emotional services, a kid who has a significant issue may need help right away.

A Concern that the School Brings to You

The advice above is predicated on the assumption that you are proactively reaching out to the school about a concern. But it may be the case that the school contacts you first. If so, the advice is to:

- Thank the school, and let them know that you will get back to them after you've had time to consider their information.
- Reflect on what the school has told you. Does it match your own observations? Is it in line with the feedback you've gotten about your child from other educators or adults?
- Follow back up with the school, and ask to schedule a face-to-face meeting. Your goal in that meeting is to listen and understand their concerns, and to use that information to help you decide if you believe action is warranted. Even if you disagree with the school's assessment, you should interpret their actions in a positive light: they are concerned for your child and want to help your child be more successful. Use the advice in the next section to guide you in that meeting.

CHAPTER 3

How Do I Make Sure My Struggling Child is Getting the Support They Need?

You've determined that your child is struggling, and you've contacted the school to get the ball rolling. How do you make sure your child now gets the actual support they need to improve?

This chapter will first focus on how to collaboratively develop and monitor an intervention plan for your child in school. While schools want to do the best they can by all their students, they are faced with the daily reality of finite time, energy, and resources. By working collaboratively and knowledgably with the school, you can make sure the right types of time, energy, and resources are focused on providing effective support to *your* child.

You also want to make sure you're doing everything you can to support your child outside of school. The second half of the chapter provides detailed information and advice about things you can do at home to help your child do better in school.

Chapter 3

How to Ensure Your Child Receives High-Quality Interventions

At this point in the process, you have determined that your child is struggling and you're getting ready to meet with the school. At that meeting, make sure you take some time at the beginning to talk through your concerns, and to listen to the school's perspective. Ensuring that your child has an effective plan depends in large part on a collaborative consensus on the nature of the concerns.

After achieving that consensus, you will develop an intervention plan to help your child. This plan could be something less formal—which is often the case for less serious concerns—or it could be a more formalized plan using a school or district template. Developing that plan might be complicated. Because a plan should be individualized to meet the needs of the specific child, it's hard to say, "Every plan should look like X, Y, and Z."

Nevertheless, there are some common elements to effective intervention plans. Use the criteria below, and the questions that accompany them, to ensure that the plan the school develops meets the specific needs of *your* child.

As a general rule, effective plans should:

- Directly address the area of need
- Have a clear and sensible schedule
- Involve the right people
- Minimize trade-offs
- Include a plan for monitoring and communication

Directly Addressing the Area of Need

If your child is reading well below grade level, the intervention plan should directly address those skills necessary to help your child improve her reading. If your child is struggling to control impulsivity, the plan should directly address the skills necessary to improve her impulse control. The plan shouldn't be vague, and it should be explained to you in clear, logical terms.

Chapter 5 provides a list of the typical types of interventions that schools provide for students—you may want to give that chapter a read so that you understand different options that might be available. Then, as the plan is developed, you should see clear alignment between your child's identified areas of struggle and the details of the intervention plan. Some questions to ask the team are:

- Does my child need a formal intervention, or would informal supports be enough? Why?
- How do the proposed interventions address the reasons for my child's struggles?
- Are there important skills or knowledge that the plan isn't addressing? If so, why not?
- Why do you believe these specific interventions are the right ones? Are there other types of interventions that we should be considering?

A Clear and Sensible Schedule

In addition to having interventions that directly address the area of need, it is important that an intervention plan have the right frequency and duration. For example, if your child is regularly struggling with impulse control, a plan to meet with the guidance counselor and work on self-regulation skills sounds great. But if it is only going to happen for 15 minutes once a month, the plan probably isn't going to make much difference.

As a general rule, the more significant the level of struggle, the more frequent and intense the interventions should be. If your child is reading slightly below grade level, an extra 20-minute dose of targeted reading instruction twice a week for an eight-week trial period might be appropriate (and chances are you might not want your child to be pulled for much more than that). But if your child is reading several grade levels below where he should, then he is going to need much more frequent support for a much longer period of time.

Some important questions to ask are:

- Will this intervention occur frequently enough to address the reasons for my child's struggles? Why or why not?
- Will the interventions last long enough to make a difference?
- If my child is making progress but still not where we want him to be by the end of the intervention schedule, can we continue them?
- If my child is no longer struggling prior to the end of the intervention schedule, can we/should we discontinue them?

Involving the Right People
Equally as important as the details and schedule of the intervention is *who* will be providing it. If your high school child has generally done okay in school but is struggling with an individual class, then receiving tutoring from a student who is advanced in that subject might be appropriate (i.e., peer tutoring). But if your child has a history of low performance, then he likely needs academic support from an adult, not another student.

In elementary schools—and even sometimes in middle or high schools—it is common for teaching assistants or instructional aides to provide interventions, as opposed to classroom teachers. This can be perfectly appropriate if the person has specialized skills and training, or if your child's area of struggle does not require specific expertise (for example, maybe your child just needs an adult to help her stay organized and complete work, but not to provide content-area instruction).

How Do I Make Sure My Child is Getting the Support They Need?

The key concern is that the person working with your child is appropriate for your child's area of struggle. Questions you should ask include:

- Who will be working to support my child?
- Why is that person an appropriate person to provide my child's interventions?
- What specific skills, knowledge, and training make this person appropriate to work with my child?
- Are there other people who might be more appropriate to work with my child?

Minimizing Trade-Offs
Chapter 5 speaks in detail about the potential trade-offs that can occur when implementing an intervention—you might want to check out that section to understand these trade-offs. In brief, however, when a student participates in different interventions during the school day, it can mean that they are missing instructional experiences available to other students. And, if a student misses too much of the standard curriculum over time, it can mean that the school gradually stops expecting him to be capable of learning what everyone else is learning.

Here are important questions to ask about the trade-offs that occur when participating in an intervention:

- What will my child be missing as a result of participating in these interventions?
- How can we use time creatively to minimize the class time that my child will miss? Are there opportunities for my child to participate in interventions before or after school to minimize the time they miss during the school day?

- Will any time spent away from the rest of the class mean that my child is drifting from the typical grade-level curriculum? If so, how can we prevent that?
- Does participating in this intervention mean that my child won't have certain curricular options that other kids have (for example, reducing the number of electives classes available, or missing different social activities)?

A Plan for Monitoring and Communication
Many schools are effective at setting up and implementing interventions for kids. Where schools can fall down, however, is in tracking the effectiveness of the intervention and staying in close communication with parents or guardians.

It is important that you are clear on how the school will monitor your child's response to the intervention, and on how the school will stay in touch with you about that progress. In some cases, it might make sense to have a lower-key approach; for example, the school might wait for eight weeks, and then conduct a follow-up assessment to track progress and schedule a follow-up meeting with you (an example of this sort of situation might be a child who generally does well academically, but is struggling in a particular class for the first time).

In other cases, it might be important to monitor a child's progress on a more consistent basis and maintain closer communication with you. For example, a student who is dealing with a significant social-emotional challenge, such as depression or an eating disorder, might require a tighter plan.

Some important questions to ask are:

- How will you be tracking my child's progress and response to the intervention? How frequently will that happen?
- What criteria will the school use to determine if my child is making progress?

- How will the school keep me updated on my child's progress? How frequently will that communication happen?
- What will happen if the intervention doesn't work? What will happen if it does work?

How to Support Your Child Outside School

Here's an analogy to help explain why supporting your child outside of school can be critical.

From your own experiences in science classes way back in middle and high school (or, for the scientists among you, college and maybe graduate school), you might remember that science experiments generally have some common elements. One of those elements is a *constant*, something that doesn't change from experimental iteration to iteration. Another element is the *dependent variable*. This is the element that changes, that varies, depending upon what happens during the experiment.

If we think of schooling as one big experiment, there is a clear constant: time. If a school starts its day at 8:30 AM and finishes its day at 3:00 PM, then there are 390 minutes available for kids to learn each day. Multiply that by the typical 180 days in a school year, and you end up with the total amount of time available over the course of a school year. No more, no less. A constant number.

It's no secret that some kids need more time than others to learn; it simply takes them longer to run the K–12 education marathon. But (and this is an important but), they do have the ability to eventually make it to the finish line, if only the school can be a bit patient.

That patience is limited, however, because time is a constant. When the time it takes for a student to learn a concept exceeds the time available, the school doesn't have many options, and the student inevitably falls behind.

In other words, while *time* is the constant in the K–12 education experiment, the dependent variable is *learning*.

CHAPTER 3

With interventions that happen during the school day, educators are essentially trying to figure out ways to steal time from one place to give students extra attention and opportunity somewhere else. Run a social-emotional support group during lunch. Pull some time from a whole-group activity to get some small-group attention.

But you can only steal so much time from a schedule that has fixed 390-minute days 180 times a year.

The take-away for you, the parent/guardian, is that, if your child is struggling in school, one of the most important things you can do to support them is to give them more time. Time reading at home. Time at the kitchen table to do their homework. Time to resolve a social-emotional challenge.

The more time they spend outside the traditional school hours doing school-connected stuff, the more likely they are to be able to catch up while they are in school.

Here are three specific ways that you can use time to your advantage to help your struggling child:

- Use evenings, weekends, breaks, and the summer as opportunities for your child to participate in school-supporting activities
- Structure your child's evenings and weekends to help them effectively get schoolwork completed
- Provide your child with behavioral and social-emotional supports outside school, if possible

Using Non-School Time for School-Supporting Activities
There is a lot of educational research that looks at the gaps in educational achievement between the children of more affluent families and the children of less affluent families. This research exists because there are some pretty stark differences: in general, children from wealthier families do significantly better on just

about every measure of educational performance—standardized test scores, grades, college participation—than do the children from families in less advantaged situations.

Much of the research around this gap provides an important lesson that could be helpful for *all* parents: in part, the gap seems to be a result of the ways that many wealthier families use time outside of school.

Before children are even old enough to start school, parents in more affluent families are likely to use a wide variety of words when speaking with their children. This means that their kids already have large vocabularies when they show up for the first day of kindergarten.

Parents in more affluent families are also likely to have lots of books in the house, to read to their children, and to encourage their children to read, again starting at a very young age. They are likely to have their children visit museums, zoos, or various cultural institutions. They are likely to have their children participate in school-supporting activities during the summer, whether that's giving their kids a summer reading list or having them participate in educational camps or trips. They are likely to encourage their kids to participate in school-run sports or after-school activities.

While this section of the book has repeatedly used the analogy of a marathon when talking about K–12 education, there is an important flaw in that analogy: in the K–12 marathon, kids don't run the whole race all at once. Instead, it's broken up into pieces. Run a bit, then take breaks on the weekends or for spring vacation. And every two miles, you get a nice, long break for the summer. But kids growing up in wealthier families often keep training during their time off. That means that, when they return to the race, they are able to run faster and farther for the next stretch.

Now, wealthier families have financial resources. They can afford to pay for things that not everyone might be able to afford. But they are onto a secret that *anyone* can benefit from: use time

CHAPTER 3

out of school for school-supporting activities. Nowhere is this more important than for students who struggle.

So, if your child is struggling, try to provide some of those school-supporting activities outside of the school day (to the extent that your financial situation and family circumstances allow, of course).

Make sure your child is reading outside school, especially during the summer. And, if your child doesn't like to read or struggles to read, then you read to your child. Make sure what your child reads (or what you read to your child) includes both fiction and non-fiction. Expose your child to as much vocabulary as possible by using complex words when you speak to your child. If they are available where you live, visit museums, zoos, farms, or other cultural institutions. Check your local library or house of worship for activities, speakers, and resources. Encourage your child to join after-school clubs or sports, and participate in town-based athletics and extra-curriculars if you can.

In other words, make learning the constant by adding time outside school to help your child develop the academic skills that will catch them up.

Structuring Non-School Time to Help Your Child Complete Schoolwork

One skill that *all* school-age children seem to possess is the ability to find ways to distract themselves from working on their homework. Especially in the current age of ubiquitous electronic devices, children have tons of options for non-schoolwork entertainment, and they regularly figure out excuses to prioritize entertainment over school work.

But keeping your child focused on *being productive* is an incredibly important battle to fight.

This is especially true in middle and high school, where teachers begin to expect that a fair amount of learning will happen outside school, and where getting work done can play a large role in determining grades and academic progress.

To help your child use time productively to complete schoolwork, there are a variety of things you can do:

- **Have set times for your child to complete homework**—One of the best ways to help a child be productive is to establish a consistent routine. That might mean that, when your child gets home, they can have a quick snack, maybe take a 30-minute break, and then they need to complete their homework. Or maybe their homework time is after dinner. Or maybe Sunday afternoons are when they work on projects and study for tests. Whatever routine you help them devise, make sure they have one. Otherwise, chances are they will figure out plenty of other ways to fill their time.

- **Have a designated, distraction-free setting to get work done**—Our brains can only pay attention to a finite number of things. This means that, if your child is sitting in her room ostensibly working on homework, but music's playing and her phone is buzzing every couple minutes with a new text, chances are her homework is only getting a fraction of her full attention. It's important that your child have a set place to complete work that has minimal distractions—no music with lyrics (classical music or jazz are okay), no television, and no phone. This will help your child make the most productive use of her time.

- **Allow small breaks during longer work sessions**—There comes a point where a kid's brain will just get tired, and the time they are spending on work is increasingly likely to be wasted and/or lead to frustration. There is nothing wrong—and potentially a lot right—with allowing your child brief breaks while they work. This might mean a 5-minute break every 30 minutes of focused work time, or a 10-minute break every hour. The challenge can be to bring your child's focus back after the break, so it's important to make it clear that a "break" doesn't mean an "end" to their work.

- **Address homework frustrations proactively with the teacher**—Sometimes kids will get frustrated with their homework. Maybe there's something they don't understand, or it just seems like it's taking forever. Rather than letting your child get caught in a recurring spiral of frustration—meaning that they will probably start doing everything they can to avoid doing their homework—reach out to the teacher. It's entirely possible that the teacher could make some modifications to the homework for your child, reducing the amount or difficulty of what is assigned. You want your child to be getting value out of time spent on homework, not getting increasingly frustrated and despondent.

- **Tie privileges to work ethic**—Many parents hold off on giving their kids electronic devices for as long as possible. But when they finally break down, they learn an interesting lesson: kids will do just about anything to keep their access to those devices. Which means that you can start making their device time a privilege that depends on them fulfilling their responsibilities around the house. Now, it doesn't necessarily have to be electronic devices, but tying your child's privileges to their completion of schoolwork can be a magical solution to getting them to get work done.

- **If there isn't any homework, make them read**—Younger students often don't have much homework, and even middle and high schoolers can have periods of lowered work expectations. Use that downtime to get your child to read. It doesn't really matter what they read (for some reluctant readers, cartoons and graphic novels can be a great option), just that they are reading. In younger children, this builds automaticity—their ability to read automatically and not struggle through sounding out every word—while also exposing them to vocabulary. For older kids, reading can expose them to new ideas, get them thinking in complex ways, and continue to build their facility with the process of reading.

Provide Behavioral and Social-Emotional Supports Outside School

Of all the factors that could be causing a student to struggle, the ones that are often toughest to address are behavioral and social-emotional ones.

Now, K–12 schools have learned a lot in recent years about these challenges, and they have worked to put supports in place. You may have heard about your child's school working on "mindfulness" or social-emotional learning (oftentimes called SEL). Those are both attempts to address the behavioral and social-emotional needs that children have, and to proactively help students build skills to prevent behavioral and social-emotional challenges from holding them back.

But they are still really tough for schools to address, for a bunch of reasons.

First, it's difficult to measure these types of needs, and to understand their underlying causes. Next, they tend to be really complicated needs that schools might not have the staffing or expertise to address. And finally, it's hard to find time in the school day to work on them without taking away from academics.

This means that, the more time you can spend outside school helping your child work on a behavioral or social-emotional challenge, the more able your child will be to focus her time in school on learning.

Chapters 1 and 2 talked about some signs that would indicate that your child might be experiencing a behavioral or social-emotional challenge. If you suspect that this is the case,

Chapter 3

here is some specific advice on ways that you can use time outside school to help your child address it:

- **Work proactively to understand the need.** If you believe your child might have a behavioral or social-emotional challenge, take proactive steps to figure it out. Reaching out to the school is a good idea. If you have the financial means to do so, you may also want to work with community or private experts outside the school to help diagnose your child's challenges.

  The key is to not wait. There are lots of parents who hope that things will sort themselves out, that their child will somehow just improve or "get better." When behavioral and social-emotional challenges are left unaddressed, however, they tend to just get worse. The sooner you can work with the school, or with an outside expert, to figure out what is going on, the sooner you can get your child the supports she needs.

- **Ask the school for advice on how to support your child outside school.** In many schools there will be at least one staff member—typically a guidance counselor, social worker, or school psychologist—who is a real expert about social-emotional challenges. They will likely only have so much bandwidth, so they can't work with every kid who needs help, but they will have a wealth of knowledge about services outside the school that parents can take advantage of.

  Once you have identified that your child has a need, ask your child's teacher or even a school administrator who the in-house expert is at the school. That person might not be able to work with your child, but see if you can schedule a meeting with them to get their advice; at the least, they can point you toward some outside agencies that might be able to help.

- **Take advantage of available financial supports.** Outside services can be expensive. Psychologists, behavioral therapists, private counselors—their fees can easily run into the hundreds of dollars an hour. But a lot of communities have free or low-cost resources available, and health insurance can cover a lot of mental-health services. Before deciding that you don't have the funds available to pay for private services, check with that in-house expert at the school and see if they are aware of low-cost or free services in the community.

CHAPTER 4

What Role Do Special Education and English as a Second Language Programs Play in Supporting Struggling Students?

THIS CHAPTER FOCUSES ON TWO SPECIFIC SUB-GROUPS OF STRUGgling students: students with an identified disability who qualify for special education services, and students who are learning English as a second language. While much of the information in other chapters applies to this group—for example, many of the interventions for these students are structured pretty similarly to those for other struggling students—there are multiple areas in which parents of students in these two sub-groups benefit from additional information and advice.

One important proviso: this chapter is intended to provide you with knowledge and advice from the perspective of a school administrator, not to give you the type of fine-grained information that an expert in these individual fields might share. Nevertheless, the information in this chapter is based on direct work with hundreds of parents on just about every imaginable topic related to special education and ESL.

CHAPTER 4

The chapter begins by talking about special education, beginning with an explanation of what special education is and why a parent might want their child to receive special ed services. The chapter then shares some insider tips that will help you better understand special education's inner workings, and put you in a position to effectively advocate for your child. Finally, the chapter shifts to talking about English learners and their unique needs.

SPECIAL EDUCATION: THE WHAT AND THE WHY

At the heart of special education are two core tenets. First, that some children have diagnosable disabilities that can prevent them from making effective academic progress. And second, that public schools have a responsibility to help these students succeed by directly addressing the struggles caused by their disabilities.

This section begins by providing a brief overview of some of the key concepts tied up in those core tenets, looking first at how schools determine if a student qualifies for special education, and then at what schools do for students who qualify. But this section will move quickly to the "why": why special education might be something that you would want for your child.

Identification, IEPs, Accommodations, and Services

The first step in the special education process is "identification": in other words, figuring out whether or not a child qualifies to receive special education services. There's a whole tangle of logistics and details involved in that process, but in very general terms, identification depends on two things: whether or not a child has an identified disability, and whether or not that disability is preventing the child from making effective educational progress.

For example, if your child has an ADHD diagnosis from a physician (ADHD counts as an identified disability), but he's making good grades in a challenging curriculum, then he will likely not qualify. If your child is struggling in all of her classes but she doesn't have any type of diagnosed disability, then she's not going to qualify because the presence of a disability is at the heart of special education law.

Some parents see a disparity between how well their child is doing in school and how well they *could* be doing, and they want special education to help bridge the gap. For better or for worse, however, special education does not share the Army's goal of "Be all that you can be." The goal of special education is to help children overcome a disability to make effective progress, not to make the best progress they possibly could. So, in the identification process, arguing that "My child is only earning B-pluses when he could be getting As" is unlikely to get you anywhere; special education is typically something that only applies to students that are truly struggling.

Once a child has been found to have an identified disability and to qualify for special education services, the team (which includes parents and educators) will write a plan called an Individualized Education Plan, or *IEP*. An IEP outlines specific academic, behavioral, and/or social-emotional goals for the child, along with the ways in which the school will help the child improve on those goals. For example, if a child has a learning disability that impacts their reading progress, the IEP will identify ways to support the child's reading.

There are two big categories of things to help a child improve: accommodations and services. *Accommodations*, as the name suggests, are ways in which the teacher changes the learning environment to accommodate the challenges brought on by the disability. It could be changes to rules or expectations; for example, allowing extended time on tests, or frequent breaks throughout the day. It could also be specific resources to help a child access the curriculum, such as having large-print books for a child with poor eyesight.

A *service* is when a special educator provides some type of specialized teaching that is different from what other students receive. For example, a student with speech delays might spend 30 minutes each week with a speech/language pathologist. Services come in a wide variety of forms that can range from a special educator pushing into a regular-education class to support students on IEPs, to pulling students with IEPs out of a general education classroom into a separate environment.

Why Parents Might Want an IEP for Their Child

Let's say your child has been struggling, you've gone through a special education identification process, and the school has decided that your child qualifies for an IEP. Should you want it?

The answer is almost definitely "Yes," but with a little bit of "It depends" thrown in. In most situations, turning down an IEP is not going to result in a better path for a kid. At the same time, an IEP is not a magical plan that will suddenly turn a struggling student into a high-achiever. Like the kids who receive them, IEPs are complicated. But there are still lots of reasons why you should want one for your child if he qualifies for one.

IEPs Don't Come out of the Blue

First, special education isn't something that just comes out of the blue. When a student qualifies for an IEP, it's usually because the child is truly struggling and the school hasn't found a better alternative to help the child be successful.

If you're in this situation, you've probably experienced a lot of frustration yourself, watching your child have a hard time and not knowing what to do about it. An IEP gives you and your child a new option, a potential solution for improvement. Special education isn't a silver bullet—more on that in a bit—but it's usually a logical next step to help a struggling child.

Special Educators Have Specialized Skills

Special education teachers have their jobs for a reason: they have specialized skills that can make a difference for kids with disabilities. Depending on their area of specialization, a special education teacher might be especially adept at working with students with social-emotional challenges, they might be able to help a child with a speech impediment, or they might have a deep understanding of how to work with kids on the autism spectrum.

Your Child Has an Identified Adult Advocate
One oftentimes underappreciated advantage of having an IEP is that your child now has an identified adult who "owns" your child over the course of the year. Once your child receives an IEP, he will go on a special education teacher's caseload, and that teacher will be individually responsible for monitoring your child's progress. This means checking in with classroom teachers, communicating with you, and potentially advocating for your child in sticky situations.

While there are a variety of adults who are responsible for working with and supporting your child—classroom teachers, guidance counselors, administrators—the special education teacher oftentimes ends up being the glue that connects those adults together. Particularly for a child who is really struggling, that watchfulness and advocacy can be invaluable.

IEPs Give You Ongoing Feedback about Your Child's Progress
Most schools provide parents with report cards multiple times a year, detailing the progress that their children are making. To supplement this information, special educators will provide you with additional information about how your child is doing. This supplemental information is directly related to your child's individual IEP goals, and should target the areas in which your child most needs support.

This feedback can be invaluable, especially for children who are struggling. The feedback can feel a little "squishy" at times (more on that in the next section), but it's generally the sort of individualized information that parents really appreciate.

Chapter 4

For Some Kids, They Can't Make Progress Without It
Some children have challenges that make success in school impossible without an IEP. These could be behavioral or social-emotional challenges, or they could be cognitive challenges. As an example, many schools have specific programs for students identified with autism, for students who are non-verbal, for students with Down syndrome, and for students with real medical fragility, and those programs are critical for the success of the students they serve.

The good news is that schools and districts all over the country have developed some amazing supports for the neediest students, meaning that all kids should be able to have a happy and successful schooling experience. But a well-developed IEP and effective specialized programs are the starting point for making this happen.

THE INSIDER INFORMATION EVERY PARENT SHOULD KNOW ABOUT SPECIAL EDUCATION
Here's a real-life story that will help to illustrate some important points.

A middle school principal meets with a family who is upset about the special education process for their child. The student has a history of decent academic achievement, but has struggled with different social-emotional challenges over the years. As academic expectations and pressure increased after elementary school, the student's grades dipped. The parents see special education as a way for their child to receive extra support, but the student has not initially been found eligible. The parents want the principal to intervene.

There are tons of tricky details to the situation. The child's teachers are generally supportive of him being found eligible—they agree that his performance has dropped and that he would benefit from extra support. The parents have paid to have an outside expert evaluate their child, and that expert comes to the IEP eligibility meeting with lots of good evidence that he should qualify. Nevertheless, it isn't a slam-dunk decision: while the child is showing some signs of struggle, he is still earning decent grades, and he has had many years of perfectly fine achievement. In addition, the results of special education testing don't clearly identify a disability—there is some room for interpretation.

The parents want the principal to "fix" things, but that isn't the principal's role. Within the special education realm, principals don't get to over-rule the decision of an IEP team. Nevertheless, the principal does have some real concerns about the process and makes sure the parents know about their right to appeal the decision.

After a pretty contentious process, and the involvement of senior special education people from the district office, the team ultimately reverses its decision and finds the child eligible. He doesn't receive a whole lot in the way of services, but the support he receives does seem to help, and his achievement improves.

This real-life story highlights the fact that special education is complicated, and being a savvy parent matters. You don't have to know everything, but there are some insider "secrets" that will help you as you navigate the special education world. Here are the tips and tricks that are important for every parent to know.

The Eligibility Determination Process Isn't Always Straight-Forward

In the story, the eligibility determination was particularly contentious. This is not the norm, but it's also not crazy unusual. While there are plenty of eligibility meetings where a student clearly does or doesn't qualify, there are also a fair number that fall in a gray area.

This is particularly true for certain disability diagnoses. For example, the category of "learning disability" can feel somewhat hazy, relying on discrepancies between a student's ability and achievement (where "ability" is determined by IQ testing) or a pattern of academic struggle over time. While educators will likely use some sort of formula or criteria to help them in making a determination, these can feel somewhat arbitrary at times.

An ADD or ADHD diagnosis can also be tricky. While a physician's diagnosis qualifies a student as possessing a disability, determining that the disability is preventing the student from making adequate academic progress can feel subjective. Social-emotional diagnoses are similarly complicated. Different states and districts may vary in determining what diagnoses qualify a student for services, and it can be hard to clearly connect the dots between a social-emotional challenge and the need for an IEP.

In the story, the parents contracted with an outside expert to help support their case. This can be an expensive proposition, but can also make the difference between being determined eligible or not. A district will almost certainly want to do its own testing—and its own testing is what will most likely be relied on for a final decision—but an outside expert carries weight, especially when she participates in an IEP meeting.

As a parent it's also important to know who ultimately determines eligibility. While the decision is officially made by the whole team, some participants' votes matter more than others. A school psychologist or special education administrator will likely be the person who ultimately decides Yea or Nay in a contentious situation. When you're in a determination meeting, be sure to ask who ultimately has the final say. And if you disagree with the decision, make sure you understand your rights to challenge that decision. You should be given a handbook outlining your rights at the outset of the meeting, but ask explicitly what you need to do to appeal or challenge a decision with which you disagree.

There are Conflicting Internal Incentives for Educators when Determining Eligibility

The story highlighted one of the unspoken truths about special education: there can be tensions among educators about who should and shouldn't qualify. This is largely because there are different incentives and disincentives depending on educators' various roles.

Classroom teachers often have an incentive to support a positive eligibility decision. If a student is struggling academically, a teacher may see special education as a way for the student to receive extra support. If a student is regularly disruptive in class, that creates another incentive for the classroom teacher: a special education decision could mean that the student is removed from the class to be educated in a different environment, or might at least mean some behavioral supports that will help the student's behavior improve.

At the same time, a special education decision can mean more work for the classroom teacher. They might now need to attend extra meetings about the student, and spend time collecting data to inform the student's individual progress. In general, however, classroom teachers are often inclined to support eligibility decisions.

Special educators have plenty of incentives to support eligibility. They like working with and supporting struggling students, and they believe special education services can make a real difference for kids (after all, that's why they chose their profession). Their jobs also depend on students being identified. Most special educators will have a caseload of students, i.e., a group of students for whom they are directly responsible. If their caseloads get smaller, then a district may be able to consolidate caseloads and not need as many special education teachers.

Which leads to the final incentive: money. Special education is expensive. Districts have to hire special education teachers and teaching assistants to provide services and support, and the more intense a student's special education needs are, the more expensive it is to educate them. While districts do receive some financial support from states and the federal government, in many states the costs of special education are born largely by the local district.

CHAPTER 4

In the story, the student who ultimately qualified created an additional expense for the district. Not a big expense: he didn't receive much in the way of services, and he was added to an existing special educator's caseload. But those costs build up student by student. So, while the overriding incentive in the special education process is to ensure that students get a high-quality education, the cost of that education is often in the back of the minds of special education administrators.

Special Educators Don't Have Magic Pixie Dust

Special educators go through specialized university courses and training programs to get their jobs. They tend to have specific and important expertise that regular education teachers don't have, especially when it comes to understanding special education laws and regulations.

But they don't have magic pixie dust. Some parents, when their child finally becomes eligible for special education services, believe that this will solve everything. They've been watching their child struggle, but now the school has figured it out, and they can "fix" what hasn't been working.

Special educators can certainly have a substantial impact on students' education, especially when a student has a particularly complicated or significant disability. For a student with more severe social-emotional challenges, or a student on the autism spectrum, a high-quality special educator who truly understands the nature of the disability can make a big difference.

But a disability isn't something you "fix," and not all special educators are top notch. Just as there is variability in the effectiveness of classroom teachers, the effectiveness of special educators varies as well.

Pay real attention to who exactly will be working with your child, and learn as much as you can about their effectiveness. This is especially true if a teacher assistant or paraprofessional will be working with your child. The number of paraprofessionals in K-12 education has skyrocketed in the last several decades, and they are often used to provide supplementary services or support to students with IEPs. There's nothing inherently wrong with this, but paraprofessionals do not have the same training or expertise as licensed teachers. Make sure you know if a paraprofessional will be working with your child, and what sorts of training they have.

In addition, ask lots of questions if a special educator is going to be directly responsible for teaching your child core subjects, such as math or reading. Particularly at the middle and high school levels, content-area expertise really matters. While special educators may know a lot about effective instructional practices for students with disabilities, this doesn't make them subject-matter experts, and they can struggle to be effective when they lack content expertise.

Having an IEP can Create Preconceptions
For better or worse, educators can form preconceptions about a student when he has an IEP. A teacher may be more likely to set low expectations, assuming that a child will struggle. They may call on a student less frequently, not wanting to embarrass them if they don't know an answer. On the positive side, they may also pay more attention to a student's individual needs, or seek out a special educator with questions about how to support a student.

Preconceptions aren't in and of themselves bad things. But it's important to look out for them. To the greatest extent possible, you should want teachers to treat your child like any other child, making allowances for your child's disability only when necessary and as prescribed by the IEP. All children, independent of having or not having an IEP, tend to rise or fall to the expectations set for them. Don't allow a disability to be what defines your child in any educator's mind, or to allow teachers' lowered expectations to become a self-fulfilling prophecy of lowered performance.

This is especially true in middle and high school, when students can be recommended for classes at different levels.

CHAPTER 4

Unfortunately, parents will sometimes encounter the preconception that a student with an IEP shouldn't be in Honors or Advanced Placement classes. The thinking goes that, if a child is a good enough student to qualify for an advanced class, then why would they need an IEP? Absolutely watch out for this. Many students truly do not qualify for and would not be successful in an advanced class, and some of those students will have an identified disability. But the disability itself should not be the determining factor when it comes to class placement.

IEPs Can Be Squishier than They Appear

When parents sit in an IEP meeting for their child, they are likely to hear about measurable goals and objective progress. The language of IEPs can make special education sound very scientific and straightforward.

The reality is that an IEP, the goals it contains, and the ways in which special educators track a child's progress are oftentimes much squishier than they appear. When developing an IEP—and when talking about your child's progress relative to the IEP—make sure you ask enough questions to have a clear understanding of exactly what success will look like and how it will be measured. If the special educator says they are going to track a specific skill or use a specific assessment, ask them to show you examples. If they say that a student should demonstrate success on eight out of ten trials, ask them why it's not nine out of ten, or seven out of ten. The world of special education includes all kids of measurable data, but you need to ask follow-up questions to understand exactly what the numbers mean.

IEPs can also have lots of eduspeak in them, which can be both intimidating and oddly comforting: after all, if you can't understand what they're saying, it must be really sophisticated, right? Parents and guardians are oftentimes the only non-educators sitting in an IEP meeting, and it's easy for the educators to fall into their own vernacular. This can feel intimidating for parents, but it's very important that you understand the fine details of your child's education plan: if anyone uses a term that you don't understand, ask them to explain it.

It's also important to know that IEPs are typically developed prior to the meeting devoted to their development. These initial plans are considered drafts and can be changed throughout the meeting, but the ideal of an IEP being jointly developed by parents and educators is really a myth. And that's not necessarily a bad thing—after all, the special educator is the expert and should drive much of the IEP development. But it's recommended that you develop your own list of priorities and ideas and share that with the special educator prior to the meeting to help drive the IEP. Then, in the meeting, check to see if your priorities are reflected in the draft document, and ask why if they aren't.

Special Education Will Mean Some Trade-Offs
This point has been made before, but it's worth making again: any type of intervention comes with trade-offs. This is especially true with special education. There is a finite amount of time available in a school day, and any time a student spends receiving specialized services is time they are not spending doing what their regular education peers are doing.

This can play out in a variety of ways. If an elementary student on an IEP is pulled out of class to get reading support, they are missing the curriculum in which the rest of the class is participating. If a high school student with an IEP has a period of daily support built into his schedule, then that is time when they are not able to take an elective class, a foreign language, or some other course of interest.

Now, parents and schools make all sorts of trade-offs all the time with all sorts of students. If your child takes band, they likely can't take art or woodworking. If your child plays sports, they may not have time for clubs, or they may be too busy after school to take honors classes with lots of homework. And for a student with an IEP, the trade-offs are often worth it.

They key is to understand the trade-offs you're making, which may not always be proactively explained to you. If your child has an IEP, make sure you ask about the trade-offs, and ask the educators why they think those trade-offs are the right ones.

Some Student Groups are Disproportionately Identified for Special Education

Historically, different student groups have had different rates of special education identification. Boys tend to be identified more often than girls, students in poverty tend to be identified more often than the general population, and students from certain racial groups (typically African Americans and Hispanics) tend to be identified more often than other groups.

This doesn't mean that you should automatically be skeptical if your child falls into one of those categories and is referred for special education consideration. But it is something to keep in mind, and it's something to ask about. If your child does fall into one of those categories, consider asking the following questions:

- In this school and district, what are the identification rates for (fill in the blank that applies to your child: poor students, male students, Black students, etc.), and how does that compare to the identification rates for all students?
- What do this school and district do to ensure that students from different groups are not disproportionately referred to special education?

It Can be Hard to Exit Special Education

This last insider secret is neither good nor bad, it just is. As a general rule, a large number of students found eligible for special education services never end up exiting the special education system.

On the one hand, this makes sense. Students eligible for special education are struggling in some way, and special education provides ongoing supports to help them be successful. Who would want to lose something that's helping?

On the other hand, however, the ultimate goal of special education is to help students overcome their disabilities to be independently successful. Now, in some cases that's simply not realistic. There are plenty of kids who have disabilities that prevent them from catching up to the regular education curriculum, and they are naturally going to continue to need and benefit from support. But for lots of kids, the goal of special education is to get them to a point where they no longer need special education.

Most special educators share this goal: they would *love* to see the kids on their caseloads improve to the point where they no longer need an IEP. But it's easy for a kid, a parent, or a classroom teacher to become dependent on the supports that come along with special education. There's nothing wrong with a child remaining on an IEP all the way through high school graduation, and that's absolutely appropriate for lots of kids. But the goal should always be for a child to become increasingly independent over time, and to develop the skills and coping strategies to help them manage their disability. After all, the real world doesn't come with an IEP, and that's where children are ultimately headed.

Just keep that thought in the back of your mind: as helpful as an IEP may be, your goal for your child is for them to move toward independent success.

English Learners

This final section is focused on English learners: that is, students whose first language is not English and who are learning English in order to be successful in school. This population of students is growing across the country, and schools have an obligation to support the English language needs of English Learners (ELs).

They also have a responsibility to support parents by providing information in parents' home languages.

This section starts with a quick look at how EL services work. Next, it talks about what schools should be doing to support you, the parent, if English is not your first language. Finally, there are some important tips about EL programs.

How English Language Programs Work

The United States has an increasing number of school-age children whose first language is not English. Because schools and districts have a responsibility to ensure that *all* students make effective educational progress, they have built programs over the years to support English Learners (ELs). These programs start with identification, and then include a variety of services and assessments to support and monitor the progress of ELs.

Identification will typically involve two parts. First, schools will survey parents to identify students who may need English language support. Then, after identifying possible candidates for services, schools will use a formal assessment to measure students' abilities in speaking, listening, reading, and writing English. Throughout this process, parents should be notified of what's happening and how their child has performed.

Once a child is identified as needing English language services, the school will develop a plan. This could take a variety of forms, but the most common is that a trained teacher (usually an ESL, or English as a Second Language, teacher) will either pull the child for small-group support, or go into the child's classroom to provide support. These services could happen every day, or could happen several times a week depending on the student's needs.

A less common type of EL service is bi-lingual education. In this situation, ELs who all speak the same language and native English speakers are combined together in a class in which English is used part of the time, and the ELs' home language is used the rest of the time. The idea is that native English speakers can gradually learn a second language at the same time that ELs learn English.

Throughout the school year, ELs will be periodically assessed to determine how their proficiency in English is improving. As their knowledge of English grows, schools will make changes to the services provided to ELs, and should notify parents of those changes. The ultimate goal for an EL program is to "exit" a student from services, meaning that their English is proficient enough that they no longer require this type of support.

A School's Responsibilities to You as the Parent of an EL

In addition to their responsibility to support English Learners, schools also have responsibilities to you, the parent of an EL. One of these is communicating with you in your primary language, especially when it comes to formal documents and one-on-one meetings. In addition, schools should be keeping you up-to-date on the types of services they are providing to your child, and your child's progress with English.

Schools send home all types of communication: weekly newsletters, field trip permission slips, book fair order forms, report cards, and so on. To the greatest extent possible, if your home language is something other than English, schools should be translating many of these documents into your home language for you.

Now, this can be crazy expensive: translation services add up quickly, and districts don't have unlimited budgets. That means that, in reality, schools and districts sometimes have to be strategic in what they choose to translate. There are also a variety of online translation services that can help to make more informal correspondences—group emails, newsletters, classroom websites—accessible to parents who are not proficient in English. But more formal documents, such as report cards, IEPs, or EL assessments should always be translated into your home language if you have requested it.

In addition to document translation, schools should also provide interpretation services for face-to-face meetings. This is an absolute must for formalized meetings, such as IEP meetings or parent-teacher conferences. Again, this can get pretty expensive, but the first step in being able to support your child is understanding how your child is doing, and that's much more difficult if you're struggling through a language barrier.

Important EL Tips

There are a couple final tips about English Language programs. The first is about services, then a quick discussion of trade-offs, and finally some information about social and academic language development.

English Language Services

Different schools and districts will put together different types of services for ELs, depending on the size of the EL population, the size and resources of the district, and the district's philosophy around the best way to support ELs. It is strongly recommended that you sit down with your child's English Language teacher and ask him to explain in detail what those services will look like for your child. There isn't necessarily one best approach or mix of services—although there are plenty of experts who *do* have strong opinions—but it's important for you, the parent, to understand the details.

Ask the teacher what instructional approach he will be taking with your child, along with how frequently and how long he will be working with your child. Also ask him how you can be supporting your child at home, both with your child's progress in English and with your child's continued progress in your home language.

What Role Do Special Education and ESL Programs Play?

Identifying the Trade-Offs
The next tip follows from the first one. After understanding the English Language supports your child will be receiving, ask what the trade-offs will be. For example, if your child will be spending part of the day working with the EL teacher, what will your child be missing? To the greatest extent possible, you don't want your child to miss important curriculum or instruction that all the other children are participating in. From the school's side, it's difficult to figure out how to manage that—presumably, *everything* that happens in school is important! But your child's progress in English is a very high priority, and spending the time on language instruction needs to happen. That means some trade-off has to occur, you just want to make sure that the trade-offs are minimized.

Social and Academic Language Development
Finally, it's important to recognize that students can require many years of English language instruction to get to a point where they no longer need support, especially if a student enters a school speaking little or no English. Within a year or two, some students may develop very proficient social language skills; in other words, they can maintain a social conversation and seem as though they are understanding everything. But there is a big difference between *social* language and *academic* language. Just because your child impresses you with how capable they are of participating in a casual conversation doesn't mean they understand what's happening in their science class, which has very specialized vocabulary.

Children are also very good at hiding what they don't know. A child who struggles with English will often do everything they can to try to fit in, to not seem like they need any special support or attention. They will smile and act like they understand when they don't. They may even get pretty good at fooling their teachers, until it comes time to take a test or a quiz, in which case their struggles will show themselves. Make sure you are paying close attention to the assessments of your child's language progress, and pay close attention to the academic progress they are making in their class(es). If those assessments show that they still need support, don't believe your child when she tells you everything's fine.

Chapter 5

How Do Schools Identify and Support Struggling Students?

This chapter is pretty technical, full of information about what happens behind the curtain as schools work to identify and support struggling students. It will introduce you to a lot of educational jargon, and go into more detail on topics that were introduced in previous chapters.

The chapter begins by looking at how schools typically identify struggling students. Next, the chapter looks at the types of interventions that schools might have in place to support struggling students. Finally, it discusses the trade-offs that are important for parents to consider when their child receives interventions

How Do Schools Identify Struggling Students?

In general, there are six primary ways in which schools identify struggling students. Some of these are pretty objective and straight-forward; for example, the school has certain standardized assessments, and a student consistently gets poor scores on those assessments. Other ways are more subjective, and can rely on individual teacher judgement or parent advocacy.

Those six ways of identifying struggling students are:

- Scores on standardized assessments

Chapter 5

- Teacher observation and initiative
- Teacher or staff referral
- Parent referral
- Systematic review of student data by school-based teams
- Educational testing

Scores on Standardized Assessments
One of the most objective ways to identify struggling students is using information from standardized assessments. This could be state-administered standardized tests, but is more likely to be something else; for example, scores on a standardized reading assessment, or a district-wide math test that all third graders complete.

This type of identification tends to be more common in elementary school. When these sorts of assessments are used, there will typically be specific criteria for identification. For example, "Every child who scores below X point on the mid-year first-grade reading assessment is automatically referred for a specific reading intervention."

Teacher Observation and Initiative
This is super common: an individual teacher notices that a child is struggling and decides to implement an intervention to help. For example, a teacher might arrange for a student to come for extra help after school two times a week.

The great thing about these sorts of interventions is that they are administered by the person who knows most about the student in the school: the classroom teacher. The challenge is that these interventions are highly variable. Student performance that might prompt a quick intervention from one teacher could be completely ignored by a different teacher. And, while one teacher might put in place a highly appropriate and successful intervention, another teacher might respond to the same situation with something less appropriate and less successful.

For you, the parent, the important take-away is that, when it's just up to individual teachers to figure out how to help struggling kids, a school will likely get widely varying results.

Teacher or Staff Referral
A lot of schools have referral systems in place for struggling students. These referrals are usually reactive—for example, if a teacher notices that a child's grades are dipping, they might refer them to a peer-tutoring program run out of the library. But sometimes these referrals can be proactive. For example, the guidance counselor might ask teachers to refer to him any students who have recently experienced a death in the family, so that the guidance counselor can meet with these students before they start exhibiting signs of difficulty.

Much like the challenge with teacher observations and initiative, this method of identifying struggling students can be highly variable. It is most effective when a school has clear criteria to help teachers and staff members know when to make referrals (for example, "Please refer for peer-tutoring any student in your math class with lower than a 75 quarterly average"), and when there are clearly identified people in charge of handling the referrals and implementing the interventions.

Parent Referral
This is also super common: a parent sees his child struggling in some way, so he contacts the school and asks for help. Much like teacher referrals, this situation is highly variable: different parents have different thresholds for what they consider "struggling." There can also be significant variability in terms of what sort of intervention comes from a parent referral (if any).

Parent referrals are most likely to lead to substantive intervention on the part of the school when the parent can clearly articulate the concern, when the concern is based on strong evidence, and when the parent is persistent.

Systematic Review of Student Data by School-Based Teams

Most schools have different teams responsible for reviewing student data and taking action to help struggling kids; for example, all the third-grade teachers in a school might meet quarterly to look at how their students are doing in reading.

There are also frequently school-level teams that handle teacher or staff referrals about struggling students. These teams often include teachers, guidance counselors, social workers, and school administrators, and might have scheduled meetings to discuss students whose teachers have expressed concerns about them. These teams often have a name like the "Student Assistance Team" or the "Student Intervention Team."

These sorts of teams are most successful when they regularly review schoolwide data to identify struggling students (for example, looking at a list of students who received Ds and Fs each quarter); when they review a variety of evidence, such as grades, standardized assessments, student discipline data, and social-emotional information; when they have clearly identified interventions available at the school level to put in place for struggling students; and when they communicate and coordinate effectively with classroom teachers.

Educational Testing

One of the most comprehensive ways to determine whether or not a student is struggling is to test them using a battery of tests measuring educational achievement, intellectual ability, behavior, and social-emotional affect. This sort of testing is usually only done when a student has been referred for possible special education services, or when parents have paid to have their child privately tested by an outside psychologist.

How Do Schools Identify and Support Struggling Students?

These sorts of tests can provide very detailed information about a child's academic, behavioral, and social-emotional strengths and weaknesses, especially when interpreted and explained by a psychologist who is actively familiar with how K-12 schools work.

WHAT ARE INTERVENTIONS, AND WHAT DO THEY LOOK LIKE FROM ELEMENTARY TO MIDDLE TO HIGH?

"Intervention" is a word that gets thrown around a lot by educators, and too often it's assumed that parents know what is meant even though they very likely may not.

An "intervention" in the educational sense is when educators put something new or different in place for a student or group of students based on specific needs identified by some type of evidence or criteria. Interventions aren't just for struggling students—a teacher could put in place an intervention designed to challenge high-achieving students. But when educators use the word "intervention," more often than not they are referring to some action taken on behalf of a struggling student.

Interventions come in all shapes and sizes. A first-grade teacher might implement a catch-up reading program with some students who are reading below grade level. A seventh-grade science teacher might pull a group of struggling students to work with him during homeroom twice a week. A high school math teacher might create a new course designed to provide basic skills instruction for students with low grades in their Algebra class.

And interventions don't just have to be academic. An elementary school guidance counselor might eat lunch once a week with a group of third-, fourth-, and fifth-graders who appear to be struggling socially. Or a middle school administrator might develop a behavior contract for a student who is regularly getting into trouble.

Interventions can happen in or outside the classroom. Some interventions are administered in the classroom by the teacher or another adult, such as the catch-up reading program described above. Other interventions, such as the examples with the counselor and administrator, happen outside the classroom.

Finally, not just anything qualifies as an intervention. An elementary teacher changing an unruly student's seat assignment, or a middle school teacher giving a student some extra attention during class, do not qualify as interventions. Those are just good teaching practices. To qualify as an intervention, an action needs to be intentional, it needs to be beyond the range of typical classroom practices, and it needs to be in response to specific data or criteria. In contrast to a simple seating change, for example, a written behavior plan with a list of incentives and disincentives targeting specific classroom behaviors *would* be an intervention.

This distinction is important to point out because parents will sometimes hear educators say, "I have tried a whole range of interventions with your child and nothing has worked," when none of the actions would really qualify as interventions. It's certainly a positive sign if a teacher is trying lots of different things to help your struggling child. But there's an important difference between trying some different teacher tricks and putting in place structured interventions.

To help you understand what interventions can look like, there are a number of examples provided below. The examples are not meant to be an exhaustive list, but rather to give you a sense of the possibilities. If your child is struggling, it's good to have some examples in mind of how the school might help. The examples are organized into two categories: classroom-based interventions, and non-classroom-based interventions.

Classroom-Based Interventions

A "classroom-based intervention" is an intervention that occurs in the classroom where a student would typically be scheduled. Classroom-based interventions can be triggered for a variety of reasons—the teacher notices a child struggling, a parent asks for extra support, the child meets certain set criteria, and so on.

How Do Schools Identify and Support Struggling Students?

One-on-One or Small-Group Work with an Adult
This is one of the most common structures for interventions in elementary schools, especially when it comes to reading, writing, and math. It typically occurs while the rest of the class is working on an independent assignment, or being supervised by a separate adult. For example, while a first-grade teacher assistant reads a book to the rest of the class, the teacher might pull a small group of struggling students to work with her on targeted reading assignments several times a week. It is not unheard of for middle school teachers to use one-on-one or small-group work to provide interventions to students, but it is also not particularly common. It is very uncommon to see this sort of structure at the high school level. The one big exception is when an additional adult is assigned to spend time in a classroom. For example, a high school ESL teacher might be assigned to provide support in a math class to several students who are English Language Learners. In this scenario, the ESL teacher might provide targeted language support to the students individually or in small groups while the rest of the class works on an independent assignment.

It's possible for a student to receive a behavioral or social-emotional intervention in the context of one-on-one teacher action. As an example, an elementary school teacher might create a behavior contract for a student who is struggling to consistently follow rules, including some incentives and disincentives for following the contract. But this is not especially common.

Independent Work
Take this category with a big grain of salt because it's rare to have a true "intervention" not include regular contact with an adult. But there are some instances in which a student might participate in an intervention that is largely based on independent work.

This sort of intervention is most common when a student has access to some type of technology. For example, there are a variety of literacy and math software programs that help students to work on remedial skills. As long as they are used in a systematic way, have adult oversight, and reflect a real, sequenced curriculum, these could be considered to be interventions (conversely, plopping a kid down in front of a computer and pulling up some math games for her to play would *not* be considered an intervention).

Cross-Classroom Sharing

This type of intervention has become more common over the last decade. When it exists, it is most likely to occur at the elementary or middle school levels (high school schedules tend to make this type of intervention very logistically challenging).

Essentially, this type of intervention involves teachers at the same grade level and/or subject "sharing" students during a common block of time. During this sharing, struggling students can be grouped together to receive targeted support. Here's a concrete example.

Let's say that the third-grade teachers in a school have been teaching a basic unit on fractions. At the end of the unit, the teachers all give their students the same test. Then, over the course of the next week, they mix and match all of their students during a common math block to follow up on the results of the test. Students who did really well participate in a series of challenge activities; students who did moderately well participate in a series of activities meant to reinforce some of the key concepts; and students who struggled participate in a series of remedial activities intended to reteach the most critical content that they failed to understand (ideally with a small student-teacher ratio).

Non-Classroom-Based Interventions

The next big category of interventions is non-classroom-based interventions. These can occur before, during, or after school, but they occur outside the classroom where a student would typically be scheduled.

How Do Schools Identify and Support Struggling Students?

Supplemental Time Before or After School
This is a common intervention at middle and high schools. The most common manifestation is when a classroom teacher makes herself available to provide tutoring or extra help to students before or after school. In other cases, students might have the option of working with a peer tutor (another student who is strong in the subject area), or working with a randomly assigned teacher (some schools might have a rotating set of teachers who stay after school to help any child with their work). A less-targeted version of this might be a "homework club" or scheduled after-school homework help, when students can receive adult support with assignments.

In many cases (potentially even in most cases), supplemental time before or after school doesn't really qualify as an intervention. It can be a helpful and productive opportunity for students, and a good use of their time, but it isn't necessarily an intervention. In order for this to be considered an intervention, it would need to be part of a specific, recurring plan in which a student was receiving support on targeted skills. So, a student who stays after school every now and then to get extra help from a teacher is not participating in an intervention, just taking advantage of an available service. In contrast, a student who is scheduled to stay after school twice a week for two months to work on a specific set of deficient academic skills with a consistent adult probably *would* be participating in an intervention.

Pull-Out Support with an Identified Adult
This is a relatively broad category of interventions. The general idea is that a student is pulled out of their typically assigned space (which could be a third-grade classroom, lunch, a study hall, and so on) and placed with an identified adult to receive some sort of educational service.

This is probably the most common way to intervene with students who are struggling with behavioral or social-emotional challenges. Examples could include elementary students with poor peer social skills having lunch once a week with the school guidance counselor and working on their peer interactions; a high school student with anxiety meeting with an adjustment counselor once a week to work on coping skills; or a middle school student with Opposition Defiance Disorder doing a 5-minute daily check-in with a behavior specialist.

This category also covers a wide range of academic interventions, from the relatively mild to the more intense. For example, many high schools have something called an "Academic Support Center," sort of a study hall on steroids in which struggling students can receive individual or small-group academic support. This would be a relatively mild intervention: the adult in charge of providing the support may not be a subject-matter expert, and the support is likely to be generally academic as opposed to being focused on a specific set of subject-based skills.

In the more intense range, a fourth-grade English Language Learner might be pulled out of a portion of her classroom's literacy block each day to participate in a daily ESL lesson. Or, similarly, a group of middle school students with identified disabilities might be pulled by a special education teacher out of English class for the last 15 minutes each day to work on the day's lesson in a small group.

Specialized Courses

The line between a pull-out intervention and a specialized course can be a bit gray, especially when students are being pulled out on a recurring basis for a set period of time. One of the criteria that separate pull-out interventions from specialized courses is the curriculum covered during the time out of the classroom. Pull-out opportunities tend to focus on the curriculum being covered back in the class, but with specialized support; for example, an ESL teacher might pull a group of English Language Learners to give them targeted support on an assignment that the whole class is completing.

In contrast, specialized courses tend to have their own, separate curricula. For example, a middle school might have a math support course that struggling students can participate in for 10 weeks. The students continue to take their regular math course as well, while the intent of the support course is to go back and teach them concepts that they never really mastered in prior grades. In this example, the support course is built into students' schedules—they aren't being "pulled out" of another course to participate—and it has its own contained curriculum.

Cross-Classroom Monitoring

The last category of intervention is cross-classroom monitoring. The general idea is that a student is being monitored and supported in some consistent way across multiple classrooms, oftentimes with a written plan outlining specific supports and goals.

This is a relatively common approach for working with older students (middle- or high school-aged) with behavioral challenges. In this situation, an adult (it could be a behavior specialist, a special education teacher, even a school administrator) develops a plan targeting specific student behaviors and adult behaviors. For example, an adult behavior might be that classroom teachers will provide an individualized verbal reminder for a student about the directions for a classroom activity (i.e., after explaining an activity to the whole class, the teacher will then approach the student and provide them with an individualized reminder). A student behavior might be that the student will not call out in class with questions until after directions have been explained to the whole class and to him individually, and then only by first raising his hand and being recognized by the teacher.

The intent with this sort of plan is to curb difficult behaviors by creating consistent environments and expectations across classrooms. A plan like this will often have identified incentives and disincentives built in (a disincentive might be an after-school detention if there are more than three violations of the plan in a given day, and a reward might be fifteen minutes of free time with a video game at the end of the day if the student experienced no violations).

Plans like this usually have a point-person who collects feedback from teachers and works directly with the student. It is also possible to have cross-classroom monitoring that targets social-emotional needs or academic needs.

What Are the Trade-Offs with Interventions?

As you might expect, not everything is smiles and candy corn in the world of interventions. It's actually quite difficult to identify the students who really need interventions, to create interventions that might work, and to do all this in a systematic way.

But even when everything is running well, there is a deeper challenge inherent in any intervention system: time in schools is finite. A school day starts and ends at set times, which means that any time spent intervening with a student is time spent not doing something else. It would be wonderful if struggling students could be transported to a separate dimension, receive enough help to catch them up, and then be magically brought back to their class without any time having elapsed in the real world (sort of like how Bill and Ted learned to play the guitar in *Bill and Ted's Excellent Adventure*).

But that's just not how things work.

The Time Trade-Off

This isn't an argument against using interventions in school, far from it. But it's important for you to know that trade-offs frequently exist when interventions happen. That way, you are in a good position to effectively advocate for your child when discussing interventions with the school.

The most common trade-off is time. Building off an example mentioned back in Chapter 3, if a school starts its day at 8:30 AM and finishes its day at 3:00 PM, then there are 390 minutes available for kids to learn each day. No more, no less. That means that time spent intervening with a student typically has to come from somewhere within those 390 minutes.

To illustrate this, let's look at an example mentioned earlier.

In a first-grade classroom, a teacher assistant reads a book to the rest of the class while the teacher pulls a small group of struggling students to work on targeted reading assignments several times a week. The upside of this intervention is that struggling students are getting time with the teacher on very specific skills in a small group. But, in order to make this happen, they are missing the whole-class activity.

Arguably, the intervention is a better use of time. Because the kids are in a small group, they are able to get more teacher attention and feedback than if they were with the whole-class. But they are still missing something.

This trade-off happens all the time with interventions. A high school student misses class once a week for social-emotional counseling. A middle school student takes one fewer elective so that she can participate in a literacy support course. A fifth-grader misses social studies twice a week for ESL work.

Some teachers and schools manage this trade-off more effectively than others. But the trade-off is always there. And, after a while, this time trade-off can lead to a more serious one: a curriculum and expectations trade-off.

The Curriculum and Expectations Trade-Off

If a high school student is struggling with the loss of a family member, and the child ends up meeting with a counselor in the school for six counseling sessions over the course of several months, that is most likely time well-spent. Yes, the student may have missed some class time for the counseling, but it's not *that* much time, and the counseling sessions were probably a more important use of the time. In this scenario, there's a lot of potential upside and minimal downside.

Chapter 5

But for a first-grader who is pulled from a whole-class reading activity twice a week, and then potentially pulled again from activities in second grade or third grade, those trade-offs add up.

The point is, the more time a student spends away from the standard curriculum and his peers, the harder it is to get back to where all the other students are. Returning to the marathon analogy, it's like a struggling runner is pulled out of the race at mile 4 to work on improving his stride and endurance. But while he's off receiving an intervention, *everyone else is still running!* So, when he gets back to the race, he might be even further behind. Now, the counter-argument is that he might now be in a better position to actually finish the race at some point—and that's an important argument—but it doesn't change the fact that he may have lost ground in the process.

This doesn't mean that interventions always lead to a child losing ground. In fact, interventions can frequently help students make up ground (which is their intent). But that depends largely on when and how they are implemented. In other words, as is true with so many things, the devil is in the details.

Section II

Advanced Students

Why the Most Successful Kids Often Get the Short End of the Stick

This section begins with a real-life story.

The setting is a middle school that is hosting a spring open house for the parents of rising sixth graders. A parent approaches the principal with a question. She says that her fifth-grade child is super advanced, and his elementary school has struggled to challenge him and keep him engaged. According to her, his abilities go far beyond the typical curriculum. Finally, she asks her question: "What sorts of things do you do at your school to help advanced students reach their potential?"

The words running through the principal's head? "Oh rats!" This negative reaction isn't because the principal doesn't believe in educating high-achieving students. But the fact is, schools have a difficult time serving the most academically capable students, and the principal knows that this kid will probably represent a challenge for the school. Here's why.

For decades, a big focus of public education has been on getting every student to demonstrate "proficiency." In other words, demonstrating that each student has acquired a certain level of knowledge and skills. And the most commonly recognized way

Section II

for students to demonstrate their proficiency is by passing a state standardized test.

Many people would argue that simply passing a standardized test is an incredibly simplistic, and at times counter-productive, way of demonstrating educational achievement. But the standardized test scores are what show up online and in the newspapers, and schools and school districts tend to put a lot of emphasis on passing them.

Because passing these tests has become so important, many schools have focused a large part of their energies on those students who aren't already passing the tests; in other words, the students who are struggling academically. Overall, that's a good thing: schools need to make sure they are doing everything they can to support struggling students. But schools only have finite time, energy, and resources. If they are increasing their focus on struggling students, that can sometimes come at the expense of the high-achieving kids.

And why can schools get away with paying less attention to the high-achieving students? Because the schools already know that those high-achieving kids are going to pass the test.

So, when this principal thinks to himself "Oh rats!," it's because he knows that this parent's kid is one that the school will struggle to serve effectively. He will stretch the school's resources, and the state's standardized-test-based system won't recognize any successful efforts. After all, he's going to pass the test no matter what the school does.

This section is about the steps that you can take to make sure the needs of your high-achieving child *are* met by your school. The first chapter discusses what it means to be an advanced student. The second chapter builds on that information to help parents determine if their child is likely to be considered advanced. The next two chapters shift to the ways in which public schools support high-achieving students: both what they do in reality, and what they *should* do. The final chapter talks about ways in which parents can work with their schools to ensure that the needs of their advanced children are met.

Chapter 6

What Does it Mean for a Child to be "Advanced"?

The parent in the story at the start of the section told the principal that her child was advanced. But what does that really mean?

When schools talk about an "advanced" student they usually mean a student with exceptional verbal, reading, and/or math skills. And, for better or worse, only a small percentage of students typically meet these criteria. This can be a tough fact to accept. Many parents want to believe that their child is exceptional, and so every utterance, funny insight, or intellectual achievement by their child becomes instant confirmation of budding genius.

When trying to determine whether or not your child might be advanced, however, you need to hold two somewhat contradictory ideas in your mind. First, your child *is* exceptional. He or she has wonderful qualities that make them unique, and you should absolutely expect that your child's school will see and honor those qualities.

Second, as exceptional as your child may be, they are probably not advanced. And that is 100% perfectly okay and in no way a negative reflection on your child, on you, or on your child's likelihood of having an incredibly successful and happy life.

CHAPTER 6

When asking yourself the question "Might my child be advanced?" the biggest piece of advice is to approach your answer as objectively and unemotionally as possible, operating on the assumption that your child will probably not meet the school definition. And again, that's 100 percent perfectly okay.

This chapter talks about what it means to be an "advanced" student, introduces the types of evidence that might indicate advanced status, and looks at some factors that can complicate a determination that a student is advanced. The chapters that follow will build on the information presented here; if you choose to jump ahead, just know that you may want to come back to this chapter if a concept is not making sense.

What "Advanced" Means in a School Context

Elementary schools sometimes have specific terms to define advanced students, such as "gifted," "academically gifted," "academically and intellectually gifted," or "gifted and talented." They will likely use intelligence or aptitude tests, achievement in a subject area (usually language arts or math), and a defined process to determine who gets the label. Middle schools may use similar terms or processes, but it's not as common for students to be referred for gifted identification in middle school. High schools almost never have specific labels for advanced students: their definition of "advanced" is typically based on a student's academic performance in classes, as opposed to scores on intelligence and/or achievement tests.

Defining "Advanced" in Elementary Schools

Not all schools, districts, or states have official ways of identifying "advanced" students. But for those schools that do, they will likely define advanced students normatively; in other words, by comparing kids to each other using scores from nationally-normed intelligence and achievement tests measuring students' verbal, math, and spatial skills (common examples include the Cognitive

What Does it Mean for a Child to be "Advanced"?

Abilities Test, the Woodcock-Johnson, and Weschler Intelligence Scales).

As a general rule, the process for designating an advanced or "gifted" student will begin in later elementary school, somewhere between second and fifth grade. Students who have demonstrated high ability and achievement up to that point will be flagged to take a qualifying intelligence and/or achievement test. If they score in the top 10 percent or higher relative to national norms, they are considered to potentially qualify as "advanced." And while 10 percent might be an initial cut-point, in reality many schools will only look at students scoring in the top 1–2 percent nationally for an official designation.

Once students have been tested, either an identified staff member (it might be a "Gifted Teacher," a guidance counselor, or an administrator) or a staff selection committee will review students' information and make a final determination.

Defining "Advanced" in Middle Schools

Some middle schools will have a formal process and label for designating high-achieving, or "gifted" students. If they do, the details will be similar to the elementary level: the use of nationally-normed standardized tests, designated scores that students need to attain on those tests (for example, scoring in the top 2 percent of test-takers), a staff member or team making final decisions, etc.

More commonly, however, "advanced" in middle school means that a student is earning good grades, taking higher-level classes where they exist (usually in math, but potentially in other subjects), and scoring well on standardized tests. And it's not unheard of for a middle school to have both systems: an official designation of "advanced" or "gifted," along with a less official sense of "advanced" based on academic performance.

CHAPTER 6

Defining "Advanced" in High Schools

As a general rule, high schools do not have formal designations of "advanced" or "gifted." This can feel frustrating at times, especially for parents who put a lot of effort into making sure their elementary or middle school child got a specific label designating their "advanced" status, only to find out that the high schools simply didn't care. The fact is, at the high school level, being "advanced" is typically about prior performance.

In high school, classes tend to have different levels that designate how difficult they are. These levels can have various names: honors, advanced, accelerated, college preparatory, introductory, basic, Advanced Placement, and so on. The higher the level of the class, the more difficult it typically is to get into the class, and the more challenging the class is likely to be.

Qualifying to take an "advanced" class (whatever it may be called) will typically rest on two factors: prior achievement in the subject area, and a teacher recommendation. Some high schools use standardized test scores as part of the course placement process, especially as students transition from middle school to high school, but this is certainly not universal. High schools may also use local placement tests to determine course eligibility; this is most common in sequential courses, such as math or a foreign language, and is most likely to be used during the transition from middle school to high school.

While advanced classes tend to be found most frequently in the core-academic subject areas (for example, English, Math, and Science), many high schools also offer advanced classes in electives areas, such as art or music. Eligibility for these classes will most likely be the same as for core academic classes: prior achievement and/or a teacher recommendation.

What Does it Mean for a Child to be "Advanced"?

Evidence to Look for to Determine if Your Child Might be Advanced

When trying to determine if your child might be advanced, the first category of information to look at is evaluative information from educators with direct knowledge of your child: scores on tests, report card grades, teacher comments on assignments or report cards, and so on. The next category is comparative information; in other words, how your child compares to other kids. Teachers may provide you with comparative information if you ask, but you will also get comparative information through state- or nationally-normed standardized test scores.

And, if you really want to know if your child is advanced, you can turn to the true professionals: psychologists who can administer nationally normed intelligence and achievement tests. But going that route can be expensive and not necessarily change anything in your child's school.

Evaluative Information

Advanced children score consistently highly on most class assignments and assessments from a young age. In a letter grading system, an advanced child will consistently earn "A"s across his classes. In a standards-based grading system, an advanced child will consistently be meeting standards throughout the year, and likely exceeding standards by the end of the year.

So, if your child is a straight-"A" student who almost always receives very positive feedback on report cards; if your child regularly gets comments from the teacher on class work that he is excelling; and if your child consistently does well on all types of classroom assessments—quizzes, tests, projects, presentations—then your child may very well be advanced. The converse—your child does not consistently earn good grades and does not regularly do well on classroom assessments—does not *necessarily* mean that your child is not advanced, but it certainly reduces the probability.

Chapter 6

Comparative Information

Evaluative information is important, but it doesn't give you the full picture. For example, if almost every student in a class receives an "A," then that "A" doesn't tell you much. This is where comparative information comes in.

One question to ask a teacher in a parent-teacher conference is, "How does my child compare generally in terms of ability and achievement to other kids?" The teacher may squirm a bit—teachers don't generally like to compare kids to each other when talking to parents—but many teachers will still answer the question. If you hear that your child is a top performer who understands and applies concepts easily, and who generally achieves at a high rate compared to peers, then your child may very well be advanced.

Aside from teacher observations, however, one of the most powerful pieces of comparative information is standardized test scores. Many children will not have taken a standardized test until they get to third grade (federal regulations encourage states to begin standardized testing at that point), so this probably won't apply to young children. But once your child begins taking standardized tests, you will likely get a report that tells you how your child scored relative to other students. This will typically be shown as a percentile. For example, if your child scores in the 86th percentile, that means that your child scored higher than 86 percent of the other students taking the same test (which is probably a state-wide population, but could be a larger population if the same test is given in multiple states).

Most states have standardized tests that they administer regularly in multiple subjects, and there are a variety of standardized assessments that children might take in middle or high school, including the ACT, the PSAT, the SAT, and Advanced Placement tests. If your child regularly scores in the 90th percentile or higher on standardized tests given to large groups of students (in other words, your child scores this highly over multiple years), then your child may very well be advanced. Conversely, not scoring highly on standardized tests is almost definitely a sign that your child would not meet a school's definition of "gifted"; remember, high scores on standardized intelligence or aptitude tests and achievement tests are the biggest component in determining "gifted" status.

At the same time, students who score well on standardized tests but below the 90th percentile may not be considered "gifted," but could still end up taking advanced classes in middle school and high school if they have also earned high grades in those subjects.

Professional Testing

If you are absolutely gung-ho to determine if your child is "advanced," then you can take your child to a psychologist who conducts intelligence testing. The psychologist will have your child take a battery of tests, and at the end of it the psychologist will produce a written report that provides both fine-grained details, and a big-picture IQ score.

There is no one absolute IQ score that guarantees eligibility as an "advanced" or "gifted" students, but your child would probably need to score in at least the 125 to 130 range to be considered. And that is on the low end: if a state or school district has tight criteria for eligibility, then IQ scores above 130 may be necessary for consideration.

Random Variables that Can Impact Your Child's "Advanced"-ness

While it's important to be unemotional and look at objective information in thinking about whether or not your child might be advanced, there are also some squishier factors to consider. The following, more random variables could impact the likelihood that your child will present as advanced.

CHAPTER 6

Gender Differences
This begins with a big proviso: while there are some gender-based academic achievement patterns that can occur in schools, they represent broad generalizations and don't speak to individual students' situations. So, take what is described here with an especially large grain of salt (and important note: there are no recognized gender differences when it comes to measuring overall intelligence).

As a general rule, girls can sometimes over-perform in elementary and middle school, relative to their academic abilities, and boys can sometimes under-perform. A part of being successful in school is following rules: paying attention, diligently completing work that is assigned, controlling one's behavior, and so on. Again, as a broad generalization, girls tend to be better than boys at following the adult-driven social rules of school, and this can impact boys' relative academic performance and teachers' evaluations of their potential.

Some boys who show evidence in elementary and middle school of being exceptionally bright can nevertheless be considered "lazy" or "unmotivated" by their teachers. Then, when they get to high school, they suddenly kick things into gear and surge academically. As they mature, and as their brains start developing the executive functioning skills that are so important in school (skills like planning, managing time, and setting priorities, skills that girls' more-swiftly-maturing brains tend to develop earlier than boys), these lazy boys who used to think about nothing but sports, skate boarding, and video games begin to turn into responsible young men who finally realize their intellectual potential.

Conversely, some girls who are dutiful, organized, and high-performing students in elementary school can then struggle to maintain that performance as they get to middle and high school. Their attitude and work ethic help them do well in the younger grades, but as the curriculum becomes more challenging and complex, they struggle to maintain that high level of achievement.

The point is not that all skateboarding boys are geniuses, or that all hard-working girls will hit an academic wall. The point is that, as a parent, gender can be a confounding variable that makes it more difficult to determine if your child is truly advanced.

Environmental Factors

In addition to gender, there are a number of environmental factors that can impact children's academic capacity and performance, such as poverty, the size of parents' vocabulary, or life experiences prior to kindergarten and during school breaks. While positive factors are unlikely to make a child of average ability look like a genius, the opposite can unfortunately be true: a child with strong academic ability can show only average achievement as a result of negative factors.

Especially if you are a parent living in an impoverished situation, it can be challenging to get an accurate read on your child's potentially advanced nature. Children who are malnourished or undernourished, who regularly experience high levels of anxiety, or who do not have access to books and educational opportunities prior to kindergarten, may not appear as bright as they actually are because their academic performance lags behind their more advantaged peers.

Socio-economic status is not destiny, but if your child has had a difficult childhood because of socio-economic factors, that could impact your ability to get an accurate read on your child's true potential.

Social-Emotional Forces

Unfortunately, today's kids—and especially today's teenagers—report higher levels of stress and anxiety than did kids in the past. And just about any experienced educator could tell you stories about students whose social-emotional struggles prevented them from achieving at their ability level.

For the parents of an advanced or potentially advanced child who suffers from anxiety, who has experienced traumatic events, or who has diagnosed social-emotional challenges, it can be especially difficult to get an accurate read on your child's intellectual and academic abilities.

Chapter 7

How Do I Work With My Child's School to Figure Out if They Are "Advanced"?

This chapter focuses on seven common scenarios that parents are likely to encounter as they work with their child's school in determining their child's potential advanced status. Each scenario provides specific information and advice to help you appropriately and effectively advocate for your child. While it probably makes sense for you to jump to the scenario that most closely applies to your situation, each scenario has information that the parents of a potentially advanced child might find valuable.

The scenarios build on information presented in the last chapter, so if you cheated and jumped straight to this page, there may be some concepts or details that don't entirely make sense. But don't worry! You can always go back and skim the relevant section if it helps.

Here are the seven scenarios:

1. My child is just starting school and seems to be bright—what can I do to maximize his chances of being considered advanced?

2. I believe my child is advanced, but the school doesn't agree—who's right?

3. My child has moments of brilliance, but no consistency—is he advanced or not?

4. My child appeared to be advanced in elementary school, but is not achieving at the same level in middle or high school—is something wrong?

5. My child seems to be bright, but our family struggles with difficult living circumstances—what do I do?

6. My child shows clear evidence of being advanced, but the school doesn't have a formal "gifted" recognition process—what are my options?

7. My child's school has said she is advanced—what are my next steps?

Scenario #1: *My child is just starting school and seems to be bright—what can I do to maximize his chances of being considered advanced?*

A child's chances of being considered advanced are largely dependent on academic ability, which is heavily impacted by the genetic luck of the draw—some kids' brains are simply wired in ways that make them predisposed to do well at the kinds of things schools expect them to do. Parents who hope to turn a child of average or slightly above-average academic ability into the next Einstein are going to be disappointed. That having been said, environmental factors can certainly enhance or inhibit the extent to which a child realizes that ability, and parents of course want to give their child every advantage possible. If you think your child is showing potential evidence of an especially strong intellect, there are a number of things you can do to help him maximize his potential.

My Child's School and Figuring Out if They Are "Advanced"

First, you want to make sure you are providing a home environment conducive to academic development. It's important to read to your child regularly, and to encourage him to be learning to read. To the greatest extent possible, you want to make sure that your child is growing up in an anxiety-free environment, where he feels emotional and physical safety. As your child ages, expose him to new words by increasing the complexity of your vocabulary when speaking with him. Make sure you are providing your child with cultural opportunities, such as visits to zoos, museums, a working farm, and so on. And finally, do the best you can to continue educational opportunities for your child during the summer, whether that means reading with your child every night, enrolling your child in education-related camps or activities, or visiting the local library together. Try not to let the summer break be a time of academic regression for your child.

In addition to maximizing the positive value of environmental factors, you will want to stay engaged and on top of your child's academic progress. Review academic work that comes home, and make sure you are attending parent-teacher conferences to get feedback from your child's teacher about how he is progressing. Parents of younger children often don't have much of a point of comparison to know if their child is truly exceptional, or just seems exceptional to them. A kindergarten teacher, especially one who has been teaching for a while, has a wealth of experience with other children, and can give you feedback on how your child presents compared to other similarly-aged kids.

Finally, in addition to asking your child's teacher for feedback on how he is progressing, ask about steps that you can be taking at home to best support his academic progress. Your child's teacher might have recommendations on books you could be reading with your child, activities to help your child's developing numeracy, or ways to support your child's social-emotional development. Kindergarten teachers have typically seen it all, and they are a great

CHAPTER 7

source of feedback and advice on how to support your child's intellectual and academic growth.

Scenario #2: I believe my child is advanced, but the school doesn't agree—who's right?

Parents can sometimes be convinced that their child has exceptional academic ability, even when the objective evidence doesn't support that conviction. There can be a variety of possible reasons for this.

Some parents really care about status. They see "gifted" and "advanced" as elite labels that mean their child (and maybe them, by proxy) is exceptional, and so they want the label whether their child deserves it or not. Other parents suspect that a "gifted" designation can get their kid on a long-term and exclusive academic track, and they want to give their child the most competitive edge they can. Still other parents legitimately believe that their child deserves the label, and they don't understand why the school doesn't see the exceptional ability that they observe.

If you think your child is advanced and the school doesn't agree, the first (and hardest) thing you need to do is be honest with yourself. When it gets right down to it, what are your real motives? If you want the status, or if you want the competitive edge, you can certainly choose to advocate for your child. But chances are the school is going to push back hard.

If, on the other hand, you legitimately believe that your child is advanced, and you don't understand why the school doesn't agree, there are a couple recommended steps. First, make sure you understand the school's criteria and process in-depth. Is the school using an intelligence test to determine "gifted" status? If so, which one? Would they accept results from other tests? If so, which ones?

If your child is trying to place into a high-level math class, how does the school decide who gets in, and do they ever make exceptions? High schools will have a specific process that they use to determine whether or not students can take high-level courses, but many schools will also have a process for students to challenge the decisions.

Once you understand the process, the next step is to review your child's information. If your child took an intelligence test, you should get copies of the results. If your child took a placement exam, you should know how they scored. Your school may legitimately choose not to give you everything you ask for—for example, private teacher recommendations and deliberations are typically not shared with parents, and schools may not be willing to hand out copies of a placement test that they use each year—but you want to get an accurate sense of the evidence that a school is using to make a decision about your child.

Next, meet with someone who can answer your questions. If your child was being considered for a gifted program, meet with the Gifted Teacher. If your child was being considered for an upper-level Spanish class, meet with the Spanish teacher. The goal of the meeting is not to argue or bully the educator into changing their mind. Instead, the goal is to understand *why* they made the decision that they made. In the meeting, ask them what separates your child from other children who did make the cut. Ask them what your child could or should have done differently to get a different result. And ask them if the decision is final, or if there is a way to appeal or revisit the decision.

Finally, sit down with all of that evidence and ask yourself, "Do I truly, from an objective and non-emotional standpoint, believe that my child should be considered advanced?" If your answer is "Yes," then pursue your options for arguing the point.

At the end of the day, the school gets to have the final say. They are responsible for overseeing a system that implements consistent rules for all kids, and, more likely than not, the person who made a decision about your child is an expert in the field (if that is not true, if they are arbitrarily making decisions about who does and doesn't qualify, and/or the people making decisions don't have any expertise in the area, then you *definitely* need to argue the point).

So, the final answer to the question "Who's right?" is "The school." At least, they are ultimately right when it comes to deciding if your child meets their definition of "advanced." But that doesn't mean you can't go on believing what you are convinced is true about your child.

Scenario #3: My child has moments of brilliance, but no consistency—is he advanced or not?

This is a frustrating scenario. Your child shows just enough evidence of high achievement to make you believe that she might be "gifted," but is not a consistently high achiever.

One of the first things to look at is a discrepancy between ability and achievement. There are plenty of kids who can knock it out of the park on state standardized tests—which suggests strong academic ability compared to other students—but only receive average grades in their classes. If your child fits this profile, it is strongly recommended that you follow up with your child's teacher(s) to understand the discrepancy. If you hear the teacher(s) saying that your child has great potential but doesn't realize it, or that your child displays high intelligence but poor effort, then there is a decent chance that your child may have advanced potential.

In that case, the next step is to ask yourself if there are other variables that might be impacting your child's ability to consistently achieve at high levels. If you are a family living in difficult circumstances, make sure to check out the advice in Scenario #5. If your child has been identified with social-emotional challenges that might impact her achievement, make sure to read the section of Chapter 9 that specifically speaks to that category of kids. If you are the parent of a middle schooler, it's possible your child's executive functioning skills may not have yet developed to the point to allow their achievement to keep up with increasingly stringent academic expectations.

My Child's School and Figuring Out if They Are "Advanced"

If, on the other hand, your child does not consistently score highly on state standardized tests (at a minimum, scores at least above the 80th percentile over the course of several years, and more realistically above the 90th percentile), or your child's teacher(s) do not identify her as having super potential, then chances are your child is a bright kid with some academic strengths, but not the level of ability typically associated with being "gifted" or "advanced."

In that case, your short-term goal is to make sure that your child doesn't slow down in areas of heightened skill. Your long-term goal, however, is more specific and is focused on the end of middle school: you want your child to have a great eighth-grade experience, because this sets her up to take advanced courses in high school in her areas of strength (remember, high schools don't care about labels, they care about prior performance). This is especially true in math, because eighth-grade math is typically a gateway course to an advanced high school math program. To get to that great eighth-grade experience, you need to:

- Have regular conversations with your child's elementary and middle school teachers about how to challenge and stretch her in her areas of academic strength.
- Monitor areas in which your child is not high-achieving and make sure she continues to make good progress there as well.
- If there are random variables that could be impacting your child's performance—such as socio-economic factors or social-emotional challenges—reach out to your child's school to see if they can be supporting your child to overcome those challenges.

CHAPTER 7

Scenario #4: My child appeared to be advanced in elementary school, but is not achieving at the same level in middle or high school—is something wrong?

There are three probable reasons for what is happening with your child: the impact of environmental factors, missing study skills, or a bright-but-not-exceptional level of ability.

In the first case, environmental factors may very well be impacting your child's intellectual progress. This could be difficult living circumstances because of poverty, various social emotional challenges, or late-developing executive functioning skills. If you are a family living in difficult circumstances, make sure to check out the advice in Scenario #5. If your child has been identified with social-emotional challenges that might impact her achievement, make sure to read the section of Chapter 9 that specifically speaks to that category of kids. If you suspect that your child's executive functioning skills may be holding her back, Chapter 9 has some help for you as well.

Secondly, your child may have exceptional ability, but never learned good study skills in earlier grades. Unfortunately, it is not uncommon to see a super smart kid skate by in elementary and early middle school, never needing to learn how to study because everything comes easily. Then, when the amount and complexity of work increase in later middle and high school, they don't have the study skills to succeed at the same level. If this might be true for your child, it is important to stress to them that they haven't failed in some way, they just have some new skills to work on. It's entirely possible that, with an improved ability in how to study, their performance could improve.

And finally, it's possible that your child is bright, but not exceptional. As the curriculum and academic expectations increase, your child's good-but-not-great ability is having a hard time keeping up. The fact is that, as kids progress from elementary to middle to high school, the academic bar keeps getting raised. Concepts become more challenging, the pace of learning can speed up, and students have to manage the various expectations of multiple teachers. Especially as kids get to high school and classes can become leveled, the bright-but-not-super students get to a point where the highest-level classes might simply be beyond their ability to experience consistent success.

Feedback from your child's teachers, along with scores from standardized tests, can help you determine which of the three cases is more likely. Make sure to ask your child's teachers about how your child compares to other students, and ask specifically if they see your child as super-advanced, or merely bright and above-average.

In addition to feedback from the teachers, review scores on standardized tests. At the end of elementary school and the first years of middle school, is your child scoring above the 80th percentile year after year (and, if they are truly super, above the 90th percentile)? If not, then your child is likely starting to hit some academic limits.

If that is the case—your child is feeling the strain of more challenging academic material and pace—here is some advice:

- Don't write off higher-level courses. It is better to struggle a bit in a challenging class than to coast in an easier class. There is, however, a fine line—you don't want your child to drown in material that is over her head in a class with kids who are able to keep up. Ask for honest advice from your child's teachers when deciding which classes she should take, especially as she transitions to high school. But some challenge is typically a good thing.
- Remember that academic ability is not fixed, and know that not all classes are created equal. Your child might love Biology but struggle in Chemistry, or excel in Geometry but curse Calculus. Encourage your child to pursue higher-level courses when they align with an area of interest and/or strength. Again, look to teachers

for recommendations on where this would be most appropriate.

- Especially in high school, higher-level classes typically mean more work. You want your child to have a reasonable schedule that allows her to also participate in areas of passion or interest, such as sports or other extracurriculars. Encourage her to push herself academically in areas of strength, but if she stretches herself with a higher-level class or two, be aware that she may be doing a *lot* of academic work outside of class to keep up.
- From a college admissions standpoint, it is valuable to show advancement over time. Your child doesn't necessarily need to take the highest-level classes in freshman year to be eligible to take higher-level courses by her junior or senior year. There are lots of students who start high school in average-level courses, but they perform at high levels in those courses and are eligible to enroll in multiple honors and/or Advanced Placement courses by their last years of high school (which both helps them grow academically and looks good on a transcript). Make sure to educate yourself (and your child) about how course progressions and levels work in high school, and speak to a guidance counselor about the possibilities and advantages of moving towards higher-level courses in the junior and senior years.

Scenario #5: My child seems to be bright, but our family struggles with difficult living circumstances—what do I do?
Here's a real-life story about the mother of an incoming high school freshman. She is a single mother, and her child is a student of color, living in a less financially advantaged home. Based on his grades and teacher recommendations, he has been approved to take middle-level classes in ninth grade. But his mother is pushing for him to be in more challenging classes.

My Child's School and Figuring Out if They Are "Advanced"

She knows the statistics: children from poorer backgrounds and children of color are less likely than their more financially advantaged and/or Caucasian peers to be chosen for high-level classes. She also knows that it is better for her child to be challenged in a tough class than to be bored in an easier class, even if his grades might suffer. She believes that kids tend to rise or sink to expectations.

When this mother meets with the high school principal about her son's classes, she doesn't try to shame the principal into putting her child into classes where he doesn't belong. But she makes a solid argument: her son has shown some evidence of high ability, but has under-performed in middle school relative to that ability. If he is pushed to work harder in high school, he has a better chance of ultimately being successful. Her argument convinces the principal, and he approves her child to take some classes that seem to be a stretch beyond his prior history of achievement.

And you know what? The mother turns out to be right. While her son never becomes a rock star student—he doesn't end up becoming the valedictorian, or get accepted early-decision to an Ivy League university—he earns solid grades in demanding classes, has a great high school experience, and is accepted into a competitive college. In short, his life trajectory is made more positive by his mother's advocacy, and allowing him into more advanced classes ends up being the right decision.

Scenario #2 talked about steps to take if you believe your child is advanced, but the school doesn't agree. Definitely look at those steps, and follow the advice. But for the parents of children living in more difficult circumstances, there is an added layer of complexity.

If you are an elementary school parent and your school has a formal process for identifying "advanced" or "gifted" students, talk to someone proactively about your child. That someone could be a Gifted Teacher, a Guidance Counselor, or an administrator. Be honest about what you see in your child, be honest about your circumstances, and ask how the school can support your child in realizing his academic potential. Also ask about how the school takes into account difficult life circumstances when making formal decisions about students' advanced status.

If you are an elementary school parent and your school does not formally determine "advanced" or "gifted" status, you should still find someone—the Guidance Counselor, a favorite teacher, or a sympathetic administrator—and have an open conversation about your concerns that your potentially advanced child may struggle to realize his potential because of his circumstances. What you want to do is to find someone who will advocate for your child within the system, and feel a sense of long-term, personal ownership when it comes to supporting and advocating for him academically.

At the middle or high school levels, educate yourself about the process used to determine "gifted" status and/or to access higher-level courses. Meet with someone at the school to discuss your circumstances, and to have the candid conversation described above. A Guidance Counselor is the most likely person to become an advocate for your child, so you might want to start there, but an Assistant Principal is another good option. You should ideally have this conversation before decisions are made about course placements, and you should work to establish a long-term relationship with that person.

Scenario #6: My child shows clear evidence of being advanced, but the school doesn't have a formal "gifted" recognition process—what are my options?
If all of the evidence suggests that your child is an advanced student (consistently high grades, exceptional feedback from your child's teachers, standardized test scores above the 90th percentile), but your school doesn't have a formal mechanism for confirming this, you need to educate yourself about the options for high achievers at your child's school and establish a productive

relationship with your child's school to make sure she is being challenged.

The next chapter speaks in far more detail about what schools do to challenge high-level students (so make sure to read it carefully), but here is a very quick sneak-peek at the likely possibilities:

- At the **elementary level**, schools may do some ability or achievement grouping within and across classrooms. This could mean that your child is in a high-level reading group, is pulled out of class at times to engage in "enrichment" activities, or spends time working with other high-achieving students across the grade level (this is especially common in math).

- At the **middle school level**, there may be some ability or achievement grouping within classrooms, but it is not super common. The more likely option is that your child might be in a high-level class for math (if that is an area of strength), and potentially in an advanced English class (although that is far less common). Your child may also be given special assignments at times to "extend" her learning opportunities. It is not unheard of for a kid to be able to skip a grade (in other words, jump to a grade beyond what her age range would suggest), but that is a move that is more commonly initiated by a parent than the school.

- At the **high school level**, since courses are typically leveled (in other words, there are more advanced versions of a course, such as an "Honors" or "Advanced Placement" section), your child will have the opportunity to place into advanced courses with other, similarly achieving students. Your child may also have the opportunity to participate in certain extracurricular clubs or groups based on her advanced status (such as the National Honor Society).

CHAPTER 7

Scenario #7: My child's school has said she is advanced—what are my next steps?
Your child's school has a formal way of recognizing "advanced" or "gifted" students, and your child has qualified. At this point, you need to do several things. First, make sure you understand in detail what the school means when it says "advanced" or "gifted," along with the extent to which and ways in which your child met that definition. Next, you want to find out about the types of services and grouping options that will result for your child because of this classification. You will then want to learn what an "advanced" or "gifted" status means at the middle and high school levels, and how curricular options and course sequences are likely to be affected. Finally, you should make sure you are tracking your child's academic progress each year.

Chances are that, when you are informed about your child's classification, you will be given information that explains in detail what that classification means, and how your child performed in earning the classification. If you are not given that information, or if you have questions after receiving it, here are some specific questions that you should ask of the person in charge of the program (most likely called a Gifted Teacher, or something similar):

- What tests and other evidence were used to determine my child's status? What specific skills or abilities do those tests focus on?
- What do those tests and other evidence reveal about my child's academic ability and achievement? Are there areas of special strength, or areas in which my child did not meet the "advanced" or "gifted" classification (for example, in math but not in language arts)?
- How common is it for students to earn this classification? What does it suggest about my child in comparison to other students in the school, district, or state?

My Child's School and Figuring Out if They Are "Advanced"

After gaining a full understanding of how the school determined your child's classification, you next want to understand the implications. Will your child be receiving any special services as a result of being classified? What do those services look like? The next chapter provides considerably more detail about the range of possible services to expect (or to hope for).

Next, you want to understand the longer-term picture. Let's say that your child is going into fourth grade (a typical time for students to be classified as "advanced" or "gifted"). In two years, your child will likely be in middle school (assuming that your district has middle schools that serve grades 6 through 8), and the way of serving advanced students could change dramatically. In addition, middle schools sometimes have course pathways, especially in math, and your child's advanced status could impact his course placement. This becomes especially important when students get to high school where many (or most) academic courses are leveled in terms of difficulty. While high school may seem a long way off from fourth grade, it helps to have a general sense of how "gifted" status is likely to impact later academic offerings.

You also want to make sure that you continue to stay informed about your child's progress, and the extent to which he is continuing to realize his academic ability. One good idea is to meet with your child's teacher(s) at the end of the year for feedback about what he and you should be doing to maintain his high performance in the next year.

Finally, it would also be helpful to find out about enrichment opportunities that may be available over the summer through the local school district, gifted organizations, or universities. If financial resources are an issue, inquire about scholarships and fee waivers.

CHAPTER 8

What Should Schools Do to Support Advanced Students?

THE PREVIOUS TWO CHAPTERS TALKED ABOUT WHAT IT MEANS to be "advanced," and how parents can work with their child's school to determine if their child is likely to meet the definition. This chapter now looks at what schools should actually *do* with advanced students.

The truth is that there is no silver-bullet, can't-miss strategy. Instead, schools should combine a variety of effective practices, consistently implemented from year to year in structured and thoughtful ways. The chapter begins by talking about some foundational educational concepts that help explain schools' approach to educating advanced students. It then shifts to looking at the right combinations of practices that you should hope to see at the elementary, middle, and high school levels.

EDUCATIONAL THEORIES UNDERLYING THE EDUCATION OF ADVANCED STUDENTS

Before moving on to nuts-and-bolts practices, here is an explanation of three concepts that are critical to understanding those practices. The first is the idea of *growth versus proficiency*. The second is a bit of eduspeak, the idea of *differentiation*. The third is the concept of *homogenous* versus *heterogenous* grouping.

Chapter 8

Growth versus Proficiency

The word "proficiency" was mentioned back at the start of this section. Within education, "proficiency" is the common term for describing whether or not a student has met a certain set of academic expectations. For example, one could say that a student has demonstrated "proficiency" with adding fractions with like denominators (like adding 1/5 and 2/5). That means that, according to some sort of assessment, the student is able to do the task at the level expected.

For at least the last quarter century, a big priority within K-12 education has been trying to get all students to demonstrate academic proficiency. To this end, most states have created standardized tests that measure students' knowledge and skills, and students show that they are proficient by getting a certain minimum score on the test.

In contrast to "proficiency," an alternative way of thinking about educational progress is "growth." In other words, looking at how much a student learns over the course of a year by comparing where they finished to where they started.

For a simple analogy, imagine a group of students participating in a high jump. They all jump over a bar at the start of the year, record the height they achieved, and then jump again at the end of the year. When looking at "proficiency," one simply wants to know if the students were able to jump over a specific height by the end of the year. When looking at "growth," however, one wants to know how much higher they were able to jump at the end of the year than they were at the start of the year.

State standardized tests are primarily concerned with figuring out how many kids cleared the bar. In other words, proficiency. The problem for advanced students is that they are already able to jump really high; there's no worry that they will clear the bar at the end of the year. But can their education be called a success if they aren't able to jump any higher? If it's already known that they're proficient, shouldn't the focus be on their growth?

What Should Schools Do to Support Advanced Students?

This tension between proficiency and growth is one of the big challenges with teaching advanced learners, especially at the elementary and middle school levels. Think about it from a classroom teacher's perspective. The teacher has a set curriculum that they are supposed to teach, and that curriculum is appropriate for most of the kids in the class. By teaching that curriculum over the course of the year, the teacher will get the majority of students to learn how to jump higher and higher (meaning that they are achieving growth), and by the end of the year they will be able to jump over the bar (they will have achieved the primary goal, proficiency).

In contrast to the majority of other students, advanced students may already know much of the curriculum. They don't need to grow as much to clear the bar, and there aren't that many of them. For a teacher who has a lot to teach and only finite time in which to teach it, the most strategic decision is to focus most of her attention on the majority of the kids, and not worry too much about the kids who can already jump super high.

Now, in theory, the teacher could do it all. She could teach the standard curriculum to the majority of students, while also taking time to teach more advanced concepts to the more advanced students, helping them to grow as well. In other words, in theory, she could tailor the curriculum to different kids' needs and abilities. Doing this is called "differentiation."

Differentiation

The term "differentiation" is a huge buzzword in K-12 education. It's almost impossible to attend a teacher workshop or conference without hearing it repeated over and over.

As mentioned above, "differentiation" means providing different, tailored learning experiences to students based on their academic needs and abilities. Let's say a math teacher wants to teach her students how to add fractions with like denominators. After teaching a couple lessons on the topic, the teacher gives her students a quiz and finds that most of the students still need more help, but a handful understand the concept and are ready to move on. According to differentiation, she would then figure out a way to keep teaching the concept to most of the class, while providing those advanced learners with more challenging material; for example, maybe they start learning about adding fractions with unlike denominators.

In theory, it sounds great! Everyone is getting instruction tailored to their needs, and everyone is able to grow at high levels over the course of the year. In practice, however, it is ridiculously difficult to do well.

Teachers have a ton of content to teach each year, and elementary and middle school classrooms can have upwards of 25–30 kids in a class. Trying to plan lessons that will keep that many kids busy and productive is challenging all by itself. Throw in the added difficulty of trying to create different lessons for different levels of kids, and it can feel downright impossible. Really good teachers can do it reasonably well, but it's very challenging, and most teachers struggle to "differentiate" effectively (which is less a reflection on them than a reflection on the challenge of the task).

You might be reading this and thinking to yourself, make it easy! Why not just put kids of different abilities into different classes? That way, the teacher can focus on one group of kids, rather than trying to meet the needs of such a large spectrum.

This idea of grouping kids in different ways brings us to the next concept: homogenous versus heterogenous grouping.

Homogenous versus Heterogenous Grouping

This section started by talking about high jumps, so here's another sports analogy to help explain homogenous and heterogenous grouping.

Lots of kids end up playing sports when they're young, like town soccer or YMCA basketball. When those sports first begin, everyone is typically thrown together in the same league. Some kids already know how to play, and some kids are clearly more talented than others, but they're all young and still have a lot to learn.

Over the years, however, the better kids start playing in different leagues. They might still do the town soccer in the fall and spring, but they're also on a traveling team in the winter. As they get a little older, maybe they try out for the middle school team, and by high school they're playing varsity.

These sports opportunities move from heterogenous grouping—everybody is thrown in together, and the coaches work with kids of all ability levels—to more homogeneous grouping, in which kids of similar ability level are playing with each other, and the coaches help kids develop skills appropriate to that level.

In elementary and middle schools, most classrooms are heterogeneously grouped: kids are all mixed in together. Why that is the case is a topic deserving its own book, but two big factors are worth pointing out. First, one of the central tenets underlying the public education system in America is the idea of egalitarianism: all kids should have an equal opportunity to receive a high-quality education, and sorting kids into different groups feels a lot like the pre-Civil Rights (and heavily discriminatory) practice of "separate but equal."

Second, connected to that idea of equality is the fact that certain groups of kids—specifically, children from poorer families and children of color—are disproportionately under-represented in "gifted" programs or advanced-level classes. Widespread homogeneous grouping in elementary and middle school would almost surely lead to classes that looked economically and racially "separate" (which is what you unfortunately sometimes see in advanced high school courses).

In practice, most elementary and middle school classes are grouped heterogeneously, and high schools typically have some of both: homogenously grouped core academic classes, such as math, science, or history, and heterogeneously grouped electives classes, such as art, band, or business. And while the research is not definitive on what sort of grouping is "best," the general take-away seems to be that heterogeneous grouping is good for a lot of kids (including students who struggle academically), but maybe not the best environment for high-achieving kids.

It's possible, however, to have a bit of both. For example, a first-grade class might be composed heterogeneously, but the teacher creates some activities that group kids by achievement or ability level. Keep this possibility in mind, because it is one of the structures that parents of advanced students should hope to see happening in their children's schools.

THE PRACTICES THAT SHOULD BE IN PLACE IN ANY ELEMENTARY OR MIDDLE SCHOOL

Elementary and middle schools that truly challenge advanced students will have a number of structures in place. It's probably unrealistic to expect that your child's school will have everything outlined in the pages that follow, but they should have at least some pieces, and be working to add more over time.

Differentiation and Homogenous Grouping

Elementary schools should be differentiating for advanced students on a regular, if not daily basis at all grade levels. Differentiation should happen via the challenge of the academic tasks that advanced students complete (in other words, advanced students are presented at times with more sophisticated work and concepts than are other students in the class). It should also happen through homogeneous grouping, in which an adult is working with advanced students as a separate group. This will almost definitely occur in differentiated reading groups, in which advanced students are reading more sophisticated texts and working directly with the teacher in small groups, but it should also occur in other subjects.

Differentiated, homogeneous grouping should be occurring within individual elementary classrooms, but schools that prioritize advanced students will also be differentiating on a regular basis across classrooms in a variety of subjects. Doing this regularly allows advanced students to work in larger groups with other advanced students.

At the middle school level, differentiated tasks and direct teacher interaction with homogeneous groups should also occur, although it is not realistic for it to occur as often as it might at the elementary level. The structure of a middle school schedule allows teachers less flexibility to chunk time in ways that support as much in-class focus on advanced students.

Curriculum Enrichment and Acceleration
When differentiation and homogeneous grouping occur, advanced students should be challenged with enriched or accelerated curriculum. In other words, they shouldn't simply be assigned a greater quantity of the same work: the academic tasks that they complete and concepts that they study should be of a more sophisticated nature.

These tasks and concepts could be extensions of what the rest of the class is learning. For example, if the rest of the class is preparing presentations on the history of South American countries, advanced students might be required to also compare and contrast three historical events in a South American country with parallel historical events in the US.

Advanced tasks and concepts could also represent a completely different curriculum. For example, while most of the seventh-grade students do a unit on more traditional poetry, one of the seventh-grade Language Arts teachers pulls all of the advanced students to do a unit on Shakespearean sonnets.

For the most advanced students, schools will offer opportunities for true curriculum acceleration by allowing students to participate in units of study at higher grade levels. This would most commonly occur in math, and could mean a younger student visiting an older class on a regular basis; for example, a third-grader going to a fourth-grade class for math every day. It could also mean doing some creative things with online learning. As an example, allowing an eighth-grader to take a Geometry class online because she already completed the traditional middle school math curriculum.

Sophisticated Assessment Practices and Quality Feedback
One of the examples above mentioned having advanced students do extended work on presentations about South American countries. In other words, the advanced students did some work that other students didn't. So, how should that be graded? Should the advanced students only be graded on the part that was done by everyone? Should they be graded on the whole thing, potentially earning a lower grade than students who didn't have the extension?

When students do advanced, differentiated work, they should not be penalized on a report card, but they *should* get critical feedback on the quality of their advanced work. In the South American project example, advanced students should be graded according to the expectations for the rest of the class, but the teacher can still tell them how they could have improved on the extended part of the assignment.

This is crucial for two reasons. First, it helps to push advanced students, showing them areas in which they can grow. After all, if a kid keeps earning "A+"s and 100s on everything, how do they know what to work on to get better?

Second, it provides parents with information about their child's academic progress. The importance of this second piece leads to a real-life scenario.

The parent of an advanced student is frustrated about what teachers tell him in parent-teacher conferences. According to the parent, "It's really nice to hear from teachers that my child is doing well, but I wish they would be more specific than just 'She's great, nothing to worry about!' Our conferences typically last

What Should Schools Do to Support Advanced Students?

about two minutes, and then it seems as though they want to rush me out the door so that they have more time to talk to the parents of other kids. It's like, if she's doing well, why do I even need to take the time to meet with them? I wish they would give me more specific information about my daughter's progress, so I can feel like I'm helping her, and not just standing on the sidelines."

This parent knows that his daughter is proficient, but he wants to help her grow. How to do that? Start by asking her teachers better questions to get better information. For example:

- What are the specific skills that you [the teacher] see as her areas of greatest strength?
- Are there activities that she could be participating in outside of school that would help her continue to grow?
- In what ways have you seen her grow in her areas of strength over the course of the year?
- Do you see her taking initiative to push herself?
- Does she seem to enjoy being challenged, or does she shy away from more advanced curriculum?
- What sorts of academic work habits do you see her developing?
- If there were one or two specific areas in which she could continue to improve, what would they be?

But in a classroom that truly supports advanced students, this parent shouldn't need to be the one asking the questions. Instead, there should be sophisticated assessments that stretch advanced students, identifying areas for continued improvement. And teachers should proactively provide students and parents with feedback to help them grow.

CHAPTER 8

Advanced Courses

Advanced courses are more challenging versions of a standard course. They will almost definitely not be in place at the elementary level (which is fine), but there likely will be advanced courses in middle school. This is especially important in math, but could occur in other subjects.

In math,[1] advanced students should typically have the opportunity to be homogeneously grouped by at least eighth grade. It doesn't particularly matter whether those are advanced courses per se (i.e., most seventh -grade students take a standard math class, while advanced seventh graders take Pre-Algebra), or simply advanced versions of the same course (i.e., everyone takes Pre-Algebra in seventh grade, but advanced students cover more sophisticated concepts at greater depth).

If a school doesn't have advanced courses in other areas, that's not a bad thing. But an advanced course in Language Arts or an advanced course in Science (or Social Studies or a foreign language) also isn't a bad thing.

Extracurricular Opportunities

This one is a little trickier because it can depend on supplementary funding, but it's nice to see extracurricular opportunities that cater to advanced students. This could be a math club, a creative writing club, or even a chess club. The idea is that, in schools that take the education of advanced students seriously, more options are better than fewer options, and resources are put toward extending students' curricular opportunities.

Two important points about these sorts of advanced extracurricular opportunities. First, they are far more likely to occur in middle schools than elementary schools. And second, while they certainly tend to attract more advanced students, they should not be limited to advanced students. Any kid can enjoy math, writing, or chess, and schools need to be careful that they are not excluding interested kids from extracurricular opportunities.

What Should Schools Do to Support Advanced Students?

The Practices that Should be in Place in Elementary or Middle Schools with Explicit "Gifted" Programs

First and foremost, elementary and middle schools with explicit "gifted" programs should have the same things that were mentioned in the preceding section: differentiation, homogeneous and cluster grouping, sophisticated assessment practices, etc. In addition, however, schools with "gifted" programs should have services that go above and beyond. In particular, these schools should have effective pull-out services, carefully coordinated curricular and instructional structures, and enhanced feedback for individual students.

Pull-Out Services

A school with a formal "gifted" program should have a person in charge of the program, typically called a Gifted Teacher. Ideally this person should work directly with students in an instructional capacity, especially at the elementary level; i.e., the Gifted Teacher should actually teach the "gifted" students. This is usually done through pull-out services, in which the Gifted Teacher pulls kids out of their regular classrooms at designated times. It can also happen through "push-in" services, in which the Gifted Teacher goes into the classroom and works with students in small groups. But it's usually more efficient to pull out a large group of students from multiple classrooms.

Pull-out services at the elementary level should:

- **Be coordinated to ensure that advanced students aren't missing important curriculum or work.** It can be logistically challenging to find the *best* time to pull kids out of a classroom, but it shouldn't be done haphazardly. Ideally it will happen at a time when the rest of the class is working on similar curriculum at a less advanced level. It should not happen when the rest of the class is at specials, such as art, music, or gym, or engaged in social activities, such as recess—receiving gifted services should not come at the expense of your child's non-core academic and social development. If that is unavoidable, see if your child can go to these specials with another class at the same grade level or even a grade level above or below.

- **Have a defined curriculum**. The work done during "pull-out" time could connect directly to what other students are doing in class—for example, while the rest of the class does a Geology unit, the advanced students are doing Geology at a more advanced level—but it certainly doesn't have to. In many cases, the work that "gifted" students do during pull-out time will be disconnected from the standard curriculum. This is fine, but it needs to be a coherent curriculum, not just whatever activity the Gifted Teacher dreamed up for the day.
- **Be academically valuable**. The work done during pull-out time should be intellectually challenging, encourage creative and multi-disciplinary thinking, it should be academic in nature (not just a lot of making pretty posters), it should mirror the intellectual complexity of tasks that students will encounter in later grades, and it should not just represent busy work.

One final note about pull-out time at the elementary level. It typically does not happen until students have been formally identified, which is likely not to occur until the upper-elementary grades (usually third or fourth grade). This means that younger students will most likely not have pull-out opportunities with a Gifted Teacher. That does not mean, however, that advanced elementary students in younger grades should not be participating in differentiated tasks, homogeneous or cluster groups, and so on. This work will just likely not be done by the Gifted Teacher.

What Should Schools Do to Support Advanced Students?

At the middle school level, pull-out services provided by a Gifted Teacher tend to be far less common. It is challenging for someone to have the curriculum expertise to work with students with both advanced mathematical and verbal skills, and the middle school schedule can make it more difficult to schedule pull-out time. But it's not impossible.

If your child's middle school does not have pull-out opportunities for your child to work with a Gifted Teacher, that isn't the end of the world. But middle schools that are truly committed to challenging advanced students will figure out creative ways to group students homogeneously at times, and a Gifted Teacher could certainly work directly with students when that occurs.

Enhanced Feedback

As mentioned earlier, advanced students should receive quality feedback about their work and progress, with an emphasis on how they are growing academically (not just how they are demonstrating proficiency). In schools with Gifted Teachers, however, advanced students should be receiving enhanced feedback.

This could take many forms: specific notes from the Gifted Teacher on report cards, mid-year and end-of-year progress reports, and/or an open house for the parents of identified students to talk about gifted programming. Gifted Teachers don't have an endless reservoir of time—they are responsible for testing students, working directly with students in pull-out instruction, training and advising teachers, reviewing gifted curriculum, etc.—so it's not realistic to expect that you will get weekly updates on your child's progress. But it is reasonable to expect that you will receive some sort of enhanced feedback from the Gifted Teacher about your child's academic growth, assuming your child has been formally identified as part of the "gifted" program.

Chapter 8

The Practices that Should be in Place in High Schools

Whereas elementary and middle schools emphasize heterogenous grouping, high schools tend to emphasize homogenous grouping, at least for core academic classes. They do this by having class "levels." These levels may have different names—honors, college preparatory, remedial, accelerated, Advanced Placement—and they reflect how challenging the curriculum is likely to be, the pace at which the class will move, and how stringent the grading practices are likely to be. Many, maybe even most core academic classes will be leveled (core academic classes are classes in English, Math, Social Studies/History, Science, and World Languages). Non-core academic classes—for examples, classes in Music, Art, Business, or Technology—may or may not be leveled, depending on the individual school.

As a general rule, the highest-level classes will be ones in which students have a lot of material to learn, there is a high expectation of student independence, the concepts will be complex, assessments (quizzes, tests, projects, papers, presentations) will be graded at a high standard, and the teacher will move quickly from topic to topic. The highest-level classes are typically labeled "Honors" classes, or "Advanced Placement" (AP) classes.[2] Students taking multiple Honors and/or Advanced Placement classes can expect to be assigned a significant amount of homework on a regular basis.

There will frequently be prerequisites to get into an advanced class.[3] Common prerequisites include a good grade in the prior year's class in the same subject, and/or a teacher recommendation. High scores on a state standardized test or a school placement exam might be used as criteria for entrance, but that happens more commonly as students transition from middle school to high school, and less commonly once students are already in high school.

What Should Schools Do to Support Advanced Students?

Simply having some advanced, leveled courses, however, does not mean that a high school is prioritizing its most advanced students. High schools should offer high-level courses in a wide variety of subjects, they should ensure that challenging courses have legitimately challenging curricula taught by high-quality teachers, and they should offer extracurricular options that appeal to the most advanced students.

Ready Availability of High-Level Courses in a Wide Variety of Subjects

This depends in part on the size of the high school and the operating budget. But, in general, a high school committed to challenging advanced students will have a variety of high-level courses in many subject areas.

High-level courses will typically be designated with the name "Honors" or "Advanced Placement." AP classes are specific courses with specific curricula, and can only be offered in areas approved by The College Board, but high schools can choose to offer an "Honors" version of any course.

It's not unusual for a high school to run some or all of its core-academic freshman courses as heterogeneous classes; for example, offering only one level of all freshman English or Social Studies classes. At the same time, however, students should not have to wait until their junior or senior year to be able to access advanced classes. There are benefits to some level of heterogeneous grouping, but advanced students need access to homogeneously-structured, advanced courses to truly be challenged.

Advanced Courses Have Advanced Curricula and Academic Expectations

If a course is considered to be advanced—and has the name of "Honors" or "Advanced Placement" attached to it—then it needs to truly be advanced. It should have a challenging curriculum that covers sophisticated concepts. It should move at a relatively quick pace, covering a fair amount of material (although it is certainly possible to sacrifice a bit of curricular breadth to get at more curricular depth). Advanced courses should also stretch students intellectually, pushing them to think in complex, creative, and sophisticated ways. Finally, advanced courses should have high standards for grading, in which students need to demonstrate sophisticated understanding of material to earn a good grade.

An advanced course generally means that students will have a lot to learn, and also frequently means plenty of work outside of school (reading, answering questions, writing essays, solving practice problems, researching, etc.). So, if you hear your advanced child complaining that Advanced Placement Chemistry is kicking her butt, with tons of problem sets and tough concepts, you shouldn't be surprised. At the same time, however, if your advanced student complains that all her AP Chem teacher does is lecture from a PowerPoint, never takes time to answer questions, assigns tons of homework that never gets checked, leaves students on their own to figure out difficult concepts, and crushes the class with lengthy tests that require nothing more than massive rote memorization, you might need to be concerned. Sometimes, teachers of advanced courses can get away with lazy teaching because they know the advanced students will just complete everything that's thrown at them, even if it doesn't seem reasonable.

Having compliant, get-it-done-at-all-costs students does not excuse lousy teaching. Which leads to the next point.

A "Challenging Curriculum" is Accompanied by Highly Effective Teaching

Advanced students deserve teachers who can motivate them, while at the same time challenging them intellectually and showing them where they have room for growth. Being an advanced student doesn't mean that you won't have questions at times, or won't struggle at times, or won't need an adult to show you that they care about you. A high school certainly shouldn't reserve the best teachers for the most advanced classes—no one student is any more deserving of good teachers than any other student—but the opposite is also true: a high school shouldn't dump less effective teachers into advanced courses because those students are considered "easier" to teach.

There Are a Variety of Extracurriculars Appealing to Advanced Students

High schools, especially larger high schools, tend to have lots of after-school extracurricular opportunities available. While this certainly includes an athletic program, it should also include a variety of clubs and activities in which students can participate. High schools that care about challenging advanced students make sure that at least some of those extracurricular opportunities cater to advanced students.

Common examples of these sorts of clubs include a Math Team that competes with other high schools, a Robotics Club, a student newspaper, a creative writing journal, world language clubs (e.g., Spanish Club or French Club), and so on. Outside of the core-academic areas, it can also mean an Art Club, a jazz ensemble, or a DECA Club. Sometimes these clubs may have academic barriers to entry. For example, many high schools have a National Honor Society chapter, which sets academic and civic expectations for membership.

As a general rule, most clubs should be open to all students, but there should be some clubs that appeal to the more advanced students. In addition, advanced students certainly shouldn't feel limited to joining an academic-oriented club—they should be welcome and feel comfortable joining any group that corresponds to an interest—but high schools that prioritize advanced students will make sure to offer extracurricular activities that are likely to align with and extend the academic interests of advanced students.

Chapter 8

Notes

1. Math is different because it is a sequential course in which the advanced "track" can start as early as sixth grade. The easiest way to explain this is to start at the end of the sequence.

Advanced Placement Calculus BC tends to be the Holy Grail of advanced math courses. For an advanced math student, that's where they want to be by their senior year of high school (in some cases, super-advanced students may actually take courses beyond AP Calc BC, but that is relatively rare). In order to take AP Calculus BC, students need to already have taken an advanced Pre-Calculus/Trigonometry course, and to take that they need to have had advanced Algebra II and Geometry courses. And the golden key to getting on that advanced track is Algebra I.

If a student takes Algebra I by eighth grade, then she is theoretically on a path that could lead to AP Calculus BC. If she doesn't take Algebra I in eighth grade, then getting to AP Calculus by senior year is much more difficult. And, a student gets to eighth grade Algebra by doing well in sixth- and seventh-grade math.

Not every advanced kid needs to take AP Calculus BC—Calculus of any sort by the end of high school is certainly an achievement. But for advanced math students, that tends to be what they are working towards, and it is a path that has to start early if it is going to be possible. And it requires good grades and honors classes along the way. No other subject is quite as track-based and stringent.

2. One quick extra bit of information about AP classes. These are classes that have a defined curriculum set by an organization called The College Board. Before a high school can offer a class called "Advanced Placement," it has to submit a syllabus to The College Board ensuring that the curriculum follows their guidelines, and teachers teaching an AP class may need to participate in special training to do so. Students who take an AP class then take an exam from The College Board at the end of the course, and their scores (rated on a scale from 1 to 5) are reported to the colleges or universities of the student's choosing. Many colleges and universities award outright college credit to students if they score highly on AP exams, and a good score on an AP exam can place a student into a higher-level college course when they matriculate. As a general rule, Advanced Placement courses are considered to be highly rigorous, and they are seen by colleges as proof that a student has done advanced work.

3. Some high schools do not have prerequisites for high-level classes, and there is a push in K-12 education to limit the barriers to taking Advanced Placement classes. This has cons and pros. When any student can take an advanced course without prerequisite, those courses can become more heterogenous in terms of the achievement and ability levels of the students in the course. When that happens, teachers are faced with a tough dilemma: do they adjust the curriculum to account for the wider range of ability and achievement levels, thereby potentially reducing the level of challenge for the most advanced students; or do they stick to the curriculum, creating the possibility that a chunk of students might fail?

What Should Schools Do to Support Advanced Students?

On the flip side, the parents of students of color or of students from disadvantaged backgrounds would likely argue that their children are under-represented in AP courses, and that by removing barriers to entry, pubic schools give more students the opportunity to challenge themselves and grow academically.

Whatever side of the fence you fall on, the fact remains that most high schools have prerequisites for taking high-level courses, but there are some high schools that buck that trend.

CHAPTER 9

How Do I Advocate for My Advanced Child?

THE LAST CHAPTER LOOKED IN DETAIL AT THE TYPES OF SERvices that schools should offer for advanced students. This chapter will focus on how to advocate to get those services.

The chapter is broken into three sections. The first section will cover the general process for advocacy: who to talk to and how to talk to them. The next section looks at the non-traditional advanced student. There are special considerations when advocating for an advanced child in non-core subject areas (such as art or music), or when advocating for an advanced child with an identified disability, with social-emotional challenges, or with weak executive functioning skills.

The final section will provide you with advice on how to advocate for general programs or practices for advanced students. In some cases, it's just not enough to advocate for *your* individual child; instead, you need to look at the bigger picture and advocate at a larger level.

THE PROCESS TO ADVOCATE FOR YOUR ADVANCED CHILD

This section starts with a reminder: effective advocacy rests on you having an accurate picture of your child's strengths and weaknesses. Unfortunately, there are some parents who are convinced

Chapter 9

that their child is on the fast-track to Harvard, and no amount of evidence to the contrary can change their minds. Make sure you base *your* advocacy in facts and information that reflect the reality of your child's situation and needs. If you didn't already read Chapters 6 and 7, it's recommended you do so: they speak specifically to this topic.

With that proviso out of the way, it's important to understand the process you should follow to advocate for your child. The last chapter talked about the *what*—what schools should do for advanced students. This section focuses on the *how*—how to get those services.

The process starts with having good information. You want to know what sorts of services *should* be available for advanced students, and the extent to which your child is receiving or could receive those services.

So, start by finding out what services should be in place. If your child is at the elementary or middle school level and there is a Gifted Teacher, talk to him. If there is no Gifted Teacher, the best person to speak with is an Assistant Principal or the Principal. At the high school level, a guidance counselor is the right contact point (or department chair, if you are focused on a specific subject area and one exists).

You should approach this conversation solely as a fact-finding mission: your job is to ask questions, to listen, and to build a positive relationship. Be super-polite, appreciative of the person's time, and careful not to come across as judgmental or demanding.

Once you have a sense of what's available, you want to know if your child is receiving those services. Again, if there is a Gifted program at the school, talk to the Gifted teacher: they would either be providing the services (for example, if there is a pull-out program), or be coordinating the services. If there is no Gifted program, you need to talk to the classroom teacher.

At this point, one of three situations will likely be true. Read through the scenarios below and, depending on the one that applies to you, use the advice to figure out the next procedural steps you should follow.

There Are Services or Practices that Should be in Place, Your Child is Receiving Them, and You Are Happy with Their Implementation

This is the ideal scenario: your advanced child is receiving services, and you're happy with the way they're working out. Hurray! You will want to keep an eye on things from year to year—the quality of services can vary as your child has different teachers—but be happy that you are in a good place.

There Are Services or Practices that Should be in Place, But Your Child Isn't Receiving Them

There are two possible reasons why this could be happening. The first reason is that the teacher or school doesn't think that your child qualifies for advanced services. If this is the case, reread Chapter 7, which has specific advice for situations in which you think your child is advanced, but the school may not agree.

The second reason is that someone may not be doing their job, and the most likely culprit is the classroom teacher. If that is the case, you need to meet with the teacher, and this may be a somewhat uncomfortable meeting. You should still be polite, but you need to clearly point out your understanding of the practices that are supposed to be happening in the school, based on your interview with the Gifted Teacher, administrator, or guidance counselor. You then need to formally ask the teacher to make sure those practices are happening with your advanced child.

Your goal is to leave the meeting with a plan in place. If that happens, that's a good step. Send a follow-up e-mail to the teacher, reiterating what you understand the plan to be, and thank her for her efforts. Then, give the plan some time to be implemented. If things go well, make sure to check in and thank the teacher. If the plan does not end up being implemented, follow up with the teacher to understand why.

If you leave the meeting without an understanding, you should still send a polite follow-up e-mail thanking the teacher for her time, and in the e-mail you need to record (again, politely) what you requested and why you believe this plan is in keeping with the school's expectations. Let the teacher know that you will be following up with the appropriate staff to make sure you accurately understand the school's expectations, and to understand what services can be put in place for your child.

Next, follow up with the school-level staff member from your initial meeting (Gifted Teacher or administrator). Review with that person what happened in your meeting with the teacher, and the plan that you requested for your child. As long as that plan is in keeping with school-level expectations, it now becomes the school's responsibility to ensure that the plan is implemented. You should follow up with the school-level staff member within two weeks to find out what is being done to implement the plan with your child. If the teacher continues to refuse to implement the plan, you need to meet with the school principal. Explain all of the details of the situation to her, provide copies of all e-mail correspondence, and request that the principal figure out a solution to ensure that your child's needs are met.

The School Doesn't Have Any Services for Advanced Students
In this case, your child's school doesn't have a formalized gifted program, or doesn't have advanced courses available for students. That doesn't mean, however, that the school shouldn't have ways to challenge advanced students.

If you are hoping the school will move toward having more formalized programs, then there is information for you later in the chapter. But there are specific steps to take in the absence of formalized programs to advocate for your child.

How Do I Advocate for My Advanced Child?

First, set up a meeting with the teacher to identify some concrete ways in which your child could be challenged (Chapter 8 provided a variety of examples of substantive practices to ask for). Your goal is to leave that meeting with a specific plan, and then check in periodically to make sure the plan is being followed.

If the teacher doesn't want to create a plan—or doesn't feel confident enough to create a plan—push the conversation up to the next level. At the elementary level, this could be a curriculum specialist or an administrator. At the middle or high school levels, this could be a guidance counselor, department chair, or administrator. In that meeting, explain the circumstances and what you would like for your child. In addition to a plan, you want to know how the classroom teacher is going to be supported in implementing the plan. And again, you will want to check in periodically to see how the plan is being followed.

If you continue to be stymied, kick it up to the principal. Again, you want to have a plan, and you want to know how the teacher will be supported in implementing the plan. If the principal shuts you down, your last option is the central office: maybe a curriculum director, assistant superintendent, or the superintendent. Same drill—looking to have a plan put in place, and making sure there are supports for the teacher to implement the plan.

Advocating for Your "Non-Traditional" Advanced Student

The previous pages looked at ways to advocate for advanced students. But there is an extra caveat that's worth mentioning: advanced students don't come in the same shapes and sizes.

This section of the chapter addresses the needs of advanced students who may require some extra or slightly different attention to realize their academic potential, and what you can do to advocate for them. These include students with advanced abilities in non-core areas (for example, music or art); advanced students who also have an identified disability; advanced students with social-emotional challenges; and advanced students with late-blooming executive functioning skills.

Students with Advanced Abilities in Non-Core Areas
Schools tend to prioritize core-academic subjects when it comes to challenging advanced students. After all, a school's definition of "advanced" or "gifted" is typically based on verbal and math skills.

But many students have advanced abilities in other areas, such as music, art, or athletics. If you believe your child is advanced in a none-core area, here is some additional information for you:

Not Much at the Elementary of Middle School Levels
Most elementary and middle schools have heterogeneously-grouped non-core classes, often called "specials" or "electives." It is highly unlikely that your child will be able to participate in an advanced "specials" or "electives" curriculum before high school (there might be an option in middle school, but it's not probable).

Your two real options are to meet with the corresponding teacher to ask her if she is able to provide some within-class differentiation for your advanced child, and to supplement your child's academic experiences outside the school day. This could mean participation in an after-school club, such as a school orchestra or chorus, or it could mean paying for private lessons (which can certainly get expensive). Towns will sometimes have low-cost options for a child to explore an interest outside of school, but it is unlikely that your child would receive "advanced" instruction in that setting.

The one big exception to this rule can occur when a district has specialized schools, such as magnet schools, that are organized around a particular theme. If your district does have this sort of opportunity, and there is a specialized school that corresponds to your child's area of interest and ability, that could be an option to explore.

More Options Available in High School, Depending on the Size

Larger high schools will often have a variety of non-core classes, and there will frequently be options for students to take advanced courses in these subject areas (smaller high schools may not have the budget, or enough student interest to justify specialized courses). There are even Advanced Placement courses put out by The College Board in areas such as Studio Art or Music Theory.

The first thing you should do is read the high school's Program of Studies carefully with your child to see what options exist. You will also want to see how students typically progress through courses to get to the advanced versions (for example, a student might need to take Introduction to Art before they are eligible to take an Honors-level art class).

High school departments frequently have a Department Chair or Department Liaison who is responsible for coordinating the work of the department. This would be a good person to meet with to understand the various course options, and to ask about course progressions. If your child has already participated in advanced experiences in the subject area, it may be possible for your child to jump straight into a more advanced class. The Department Chair, or the instructor for the course, should be able to give you specific information on how that might occur.

Advanced Students with an Identified Disability

Students who have an identified disability that requires specialized educational services can qualify for an IEP, or Individualized Education Program. Chapter 4 talks about special education and IEPs at length, but there are some important points to make here.

First, as a general rule, students who have an IEP are under-represented in formalized "gifted" programs, advanced curricular opportunities, and advanced high school courses. On one level this seems to make sense: students that need specialized services are generally kids who struggle academically, so it would not seem that they would be good candidates for advanced educational opportunities. The thinking is, if they are able to do advanced academic work, why should they need an IEP?

But that line of thinking is flawed. While many students with disabilities do struggle academically and would not be good candidates for advanced work or courses, there are also students with disabilities who absolutely *should* be doing advanced work because they have the intellectual ability to do so. The nature of their disability might mean that they require certain supports and services to be academically successful, but it does not exclude them from participation in advanced work. To illustrate this point, here's a real-life example of a high school student diagnosed with autism.

This student frequently needs to get up and pace in the back of the classroom, and she's almost incapable of verbal interactions in a classroom setting. She meets with a special educator for a period each day to help her work on her anxiety and social skills, and it is not unheard of for her to need to miss a class because she's not emotionally able to attend.

At the same time, she's brilliant. In high school she ends up taking a number of Advanced Placement and Honors classes and does tremendously well. She certainly has an identified disability that complicates her education, and it's entirely appropriate that she has an IEP. But she's also a student who needs to be challenged with advanced curriculum.

The bottom line is, having an identified disability should never in-and-of-itself prevent a student from participating in advanced academic work. In addition, students with an IEP are required by federal law to receive accommodations, even in advanced high school courses. That does not mean that students should participate in activities or enroll in classes that are beyond their ability or achievement level. But students with advanced academic and intellectual ability should not be prevented from doing so because of an identified disability.

This can create a real challenge for parents: how to get an accurate read on your child's academic ability, and to disentangle that ability from any identified disabilities when it comes to academic performance? Unfortunately, there are no simple recommendations, but here is some advice that might help:

- **Review testing information very carefully**—As part of the special education identification process, you will most likely get very detailed testing information on your child, including information about your child's tested intellectual ability (i.e., IQ scores). Review this information very carefully. If your child has a high tested IQ (as a general rule, in excess of 125 or 130), that suggests significant intellectual capacity that might be appropriate for advanced academic work.
- **Work very closely with the school's or district's special education point person**—You will certainly want the appropriate school or district personnel to fully explain your child's testing information. But beyond that, you want to develop a close relationship with the special educator who is in charge of your child at the school level. This is someone who can serve as an advocate for your child in arguing for advanced academic opportunities, and who can help to put together a formal plan. In addition to the person at the school level, it might not be a bad idea to speak with someone in the district office who is involved with special education. If the school point-person is handling things, that may not be necessary. But having a district contact doesn't hurt, especially as your child transitions from elementary to middle to high school.
- **Seek out other parents and special education parent associations**—What you don't want to do is have to figure everything out on your own. Chances are, whatever you are experiencing at the school (good, bad, or in-between), another parent is having a similar experience. There are likely some formalized parent advocacy and support

groups for students with disabilities: see if they might be able to help. You may very well be in the minority within the group—there aren't a ton of students with disabilities who qualify for advanced academic work—but chances are you will find at least one other person who shares your circumstances.

- **Understand the school's challenge**—As stated previously, there aren't a lot of students with disabilities who qualify for advanced academic work. That means that the school is unlikely to have a lot of experience serving students in this type of situation, so it may be tough for them to figure out how to do so appropriately. That doesn't mean you shouldn't advocate for your child—far from it—but your ability to effectively support your child will be helped if you understand the school's perspective.

- **Prioritize adult behaviors over attitudes**—When these sorts of situations occur, it is not uncommon for parents to really, really want their child's teacher(s) to *understand*. To understand the disability, to understand their advocacy, to understand their child's experiences, to understand why it is so important that their child be challenged appropriately. The parents want to change a reluctant or recalcitrant teacher's attitude toward their child. But that frequently doesn't work, and it can lead to frustration, anger, and hurt feelings, on all sides. As important as it can be to you to have others understand your child's situation, focus on their actions. You may know that a teacher doesn't agree with putting your child in an advanced class, but as long as your child ends up in the class and the teacher follows the IEP, she doesn't need to agree. There are ways to change attitudes over time through long-term advocacy, district policy work, public meetings, and so on. But don't set your goal as changing the attitudes of your child's teacher(s): just making sure that they behave in a way that gets your child a great education.

Students with Social-Emotional Challenges
Many students experience social-emotional challenges. They might feel anxious in social settings, have poor self-esteem or a negative self-image, withdraw emotionally during a divorce or in the wake of a family death, get involved in substance abuse, be prone to oppositional behaviors, experience depression, and so on. A student's ability to participate in advanced learning opportunities should not be prevented by a social-emotional challenge, but there are limits to what schools can do. The first thing to consider is the severity of the situation:

Low-Level Social-Emotional Challenges
If a student's social-emotional challenge does not regularly impact his ability to attend school, to complete work, or to function on a daily basis, then a parent should expect that it will not limit his opportunity to participate in advanced curricular opportunities. It is reasonable to expect teachers to make limited accommodations without impacting a student's overall academic standing or progress. For example, a student who is selectively mute and is not able to make presentations in front of the class could be given an opportunity to present privately to the teacher.

Moderate Social-Emotional Challenges
If a student's social-emotional challenge impacts school or class attendance, but only on an intermittent or short-term basis, then it is certainly reasonable for a school to make advanced curricular opportunities available. For example, if a student is fighting an eating disorder and needs to be hospitalized for a short period of time, that should not preclude her continued participation in

advanced curriculum. It might require some flexibility on the part of the school, but it's not impossible to figure out.

Significant Social-Emotional Challenges

When students miss a considerable amount of school, or regularly miss classes as a result of a social-emotional challenge, it becomes very difficult for a school to continue to provide advanced curricular opportunities. There is more flexibility at the elementary and middle school levels, but it becomes especially challenging in high school. There are two big reasons why.

First, when a student misses significant amounts of school, it is logistically difficult to replicate the missed instructional experiences. Schools can send work home, maybe even arrange for some out-of-school tutoring, but schooling is about more than just doing assignments in a book: it is the daily instructional experience in a classroom setting with a professional educator. Trying to provide an advanced student with enriched curricular opportunities commensurate with what they would experience at school may just not be feasible.

Second, high schools produce a transcript. That transcript is a record of the classes that a student has taken, and the student's level of performance in those classes. Outside institutions—colleges, universities, scholarship organizations, potential employers—use that transcript to make decisions about students, and they do so on the assumption that transcripts communicate consistent information. In other words, if two students both took an Honors-level sophomore English class, the transcript should reflect their comparative performance in that class.

But if a high school begins making accommodations for a student who misses substantial class time because of a social-emotional challenge, and those accommodations are significant enough that the nature of the curriculum has effectively changed, those transcripts are no longer accurate. If one student in an Honors class had to do all of the assigned work and earned a

"B," and a student missing significant amounts of time only had to do half the work (to accommodate her absences) and also earned a "B," those two transcripts are not communicating consistent information. A possible solution is to change the level of the class designated on the transcript to reflect a change in expectations. But the point is that high schools walk a fine line in making accommodations for advanced students that end up changing the substance of the course and expectations.

For parents whose advanced child is experiencing a social-emotional challenge, here are a few recommendations:

Have Documentation

If you are hoping that the school might accommodate your child in some substantive way, then you will need to present the school with medical documentation. It's not unheard for parents to request that their child get some sort of accommodation—shorter tests, regular extensions on assignments, and so on—only to back off when the school asks for something from a doctor demonstrating that these requests are based on a medical need.

The fact is, schools cannot provide substantive accommodations to kids based on a parent's word alone. This is especially true given that accommodations may provide a child with advantages over other students in the class. Simple stuff—for example, asking a teacher to limit the extent to which they call on a student in class because the student experiences anxiety in social situations—likely won't require any documentation. But any request that requires something substantive will almost definitely require a doctor's note.

Work with the School to Understand your Options

If your child is experiencing a social-emotional challenge, it's recommended that you let the school know proactively. Some parents want to keep information private, which is completely understandable; some situations don't need to be anyone else's business. But many parents end up being surprised at how creative, accommodating, caring, and discreet a school can be once it's aware of an issue.

If you do feel comfortable approaching the school, a trusted teacher or a guidance counselor is a good place to start. In most circumstances, your goal in the first meeting is simply informational: you want to update the school on where things stand with your child, and you want to understand what that might mean. Some parents approach an initial meeting with a plan of action already formulated in their head, only to find out that their plan simply isn't feasible. The advisable approach is to work with the school to develop a plan; you very well may be pleasantly surprised to find out that the school proposes options that you didn't even know existed.

Prioritize your Child's Social-Emotional Well-Being Over Advanced Academic Progress

Many parents have a picture in their head of what they want their child's educational path to be, and it can be hard to let that picture go when their advanced kid encounters a significant social-emotional challenge. This is especially true in high school, where parents are often focused on making sure their child maintains a strong transcript for college, despite the fact that their child is in crisis.

If your child is in the middle of something really serious, such as substance-addiction or suicidal tendencies, focus first on helping your child get well. Your child may also have a hard time letting go of his own academic self-expectations, hoping to just quickly "fix" the problem and move on. But significant social-emotional crises require extended time and treatment with professional support. Your child's long-term health is far more important than a transcript.

Consider a Special Education Process, if the Rules Allow It

In some states, a diagnosed social-emotional disability can qualify a student for special education services. It seems that more and more schools are creating support programs for students with social-emotional challenges, and an IEP (the plan that is developed when a student qualifies for special education services) can give your child access to supports that might be harder to get without an IEP.

This does not mean that any child with a social-emotional challenge would or should qualify for an IEP; the special education identification process is lengthy and involves a significant amount of data collection. But if your advanced child has an ongoing social-emotional challenge that is inhibiting his ability to realize his academic potential, this is an avenue to explore.

Students with Late-Blooming Executive Functioning Skills

Executive functioning skills are things such as time management, long-term planning, impulse control, and organization. The part of the brain that houses these skills serves as a sort of air traffic controller for other brain activity[1], and this part of the brain (and the associated skills) improves significantly during adolescence. These skills are also ones that are critically important for school success, especially as students transition into the more complicated and logistically challenging worlds of middle and high school.

For advanced students whose executive functioning skills are slow in developing, school can become a nightmare. Teachers become frustrated with a clearly bright student who can't get work done, focus, or stay organized. Parents are frustrated as their clearly-capable child starts to fall behind academically, failing to realize his intellectual potential. And the poor kid can't keep things straight, feeling confused and overwhelmed as he disappoints the important adults in his life.

CHAPTER 9

Unfortunately, because advanced school status is based increasingly on academic performance in middle and high school, super-bright kids with poor executive functioning skills can fail to qualify for upper-level courses if those skills don't kick in until too late.

For parents in this situation, it means finding a balance at school between supporting your child, controlling your child, and covering for your child. Here is some key advice:

Do Support Your Child

One of the things you can do as a parent is to take the place of your child's non-existent executive functioning skills. If his brain can't help him stay organized, you keep him organized. If his brain can't help him plan out his week, you sit him down and plan it out with him. But this can mean a lot of work on your end.

One of the big killers for kids in this situation is simply getting stuff done, especially homework and long-term assignments. Because they are not able to plan well, these students regularly "remember" on a Thursday night that they have a huge project due the next day, and they haven't done any work on it. To avoid this, parents need to set up a calendar that tracks a child's school assignments (or get access to an electronic copy of a child's existing academic calendar through school); set up routines to help the child get work done (for example, setting aside the same chunk of time every day for academics); and monitor their progress as they work. If teachers put assignments online, check regularly to keep on top of what is coming up.

Parents should also be proactive in talking with their child's teacher(s) about the issue. Teachers may be willing to provide some in-class support, and they could have advice on different strategies to use at home. They might even offer to send reminders about big upcoming assignments to avoid those last-minute, Thursday night surprises.

How Do I Advocate for My Advanced Child?

Don't Control Your Child

One of the dangers of heavily supporting your child is that it can create a negative dynamic. If a big chunk of your interactions with your child is about schoolwork, and you are regularly in the position of nagging him or punishing him for not meeting your expectations, your long-term relationship with your child can be affected. That doesn't mean that you should never play the role of the bad guy—that's simply part of being a parent sometimes. But if a parent thinks they need to control their child's every move, that can end up playing out badly, especially once the kid gets older.

Don't Cover for Your Child

One practice that is all too common with a student in this situation is that the parents start making excuses for their child, or they simply start doing his work for him. Their child forgets to do an assignment, so mom sends an email to the teacher with a made-up excuse. Or when the child remembers that he has a project due the next day, dad stays up until 3:00 AM getting it done (while the child, of course, sleeps blissfully).

There are lots of reasons why this is a bad idea. First and foremost, it doesn't help your child improve. If he gets used to you covering for his lack of organization, he has no incentive to actually become more organized. Second, the teacher is going to figure it out, and that will likely lead to accusations, defensiveness, and a strained relationship. And finally, the school is developing an inaccurate picture of who your child is, which means they are in a worse position to help him improve his skills.

Here's a real-life example of a high school freshman. The child's father is worried that his bright child is struggling in school, so he meets with the school principal. The parent is particularly frustrated with his son's teachers, who the parent says are inconsistent in the way they publish information about assignments to their class websites. The parent complains to the principal: "It's really hard for me to keep track of all his assignments and know when everything is due. I need the teachers to be more consistent about this to help me out!"

The principal's response is straightforward: "That's not your job, that's your son's job." This dad has gotten to the point where he's essentially his son's personal academic secretary, keeping track of all his responsibilities so that the kid doesn't need to do a thing.

This highlights the delicate balance that parents in this situation need to manage. On the one hand, you do want to support your child and help him stay organized. But by the time your child gets to high school, you need to start backing off to allow your child to develop his executive functioning skills. That doesn't mean to let your child drown in a sea of unmanageable academic expectations. It does mean, however, allowing your child to learn how to manage his time by being progressively more responsible for managing it, even if it does come with a bad grade or a lost privilege every now and then.

Advocating for Programs and Practices for Advanced Students

There's an unfortunate experience that's common to many of the parents of high-achieving students, especially those in schools that don't have formalized "gifted" programs: they have to learn to live with an ongoing sense of frustration.

They're frustrated because everything just seems to be more difficult than it should be. Their kids are bright, their kids are typically well-behaved, their kids tend to like school (at least initially). But it feels like an uphill battle to get their kids the services and programs that they need, and every year the struggle starts all over again with a new classroom or set of teachers.

If this is striking a chord with you, the answer may be to move your advocacy beyond just your child. Until your school and district have formalized programs and practices in place for advanced students, you'll keep encountering the same frustrations.

Now, advocating for systemic change is harder than just advocating for your individual child. But when it works, the bonuses are huge: not only does your child benefit from improved programming, but so do a lot of other kids.

If you are interested in taking your advocacy to the school or district level, the advice below will help you in your efforts.

Start with a Need, Not a Solution
Many parent advocates make the mistake of walking into a principal's office and saying "This is a problem, and you need to do X, Y, and Z to fix it!" (or, alternatively, they type a 1,500-word email with the same message). But that's actually the wrong way to go about it.

Instead of jumping straight to a solution, you should start by focusing on needs. For example, you might want a "gifted" identification process in elementary school because you and a bunch of your friends have noticed that there's no rhyme or reason to how teachers decide which students should do advanced academic work. The "need" is that potentially-advanced students are not receiving consistent services in a structured, organized, and consistent way. A "gifted" identification process might be one possible solution, but it's not necessarily the only, or even the most effective one.

There are two big reasons to start with needs instead of solutions, one philosophical and one strategic. First, jumping straight to one solution might mean overlooking alternative solutions that could be more effective in meeting the need. Second, the moment you propose a solution, opponents have something concrete to rail against. "A 'gifted' identification process? That sounds really expensive, and simply identifying students isn't going to get us anywhere."

By focusing first on accurately identifying the need, but without proposing any specific solution, you limit the possibility of your ideas being shot down, and you increase the possibility that others will get on board. Someone may be opposed to creating a "gifted" identification process, but they agree that something needs to be done to create more consistent services for advanced kids.

Decide if you Want Action, or Awareness

If your district already has some programs and services in place for advanced students, or if you have some very specific needs that you believe should be met, then your goal might be to improve or build on what already exists. But if your district has absolutely nothing, or if the needs you identify are especially broad, then you have a much bigger hill to climb.

For that reason, you need to decide if your primary goal is spurring action, or building awareness. If there is a concrete need that could be met with some specific district-level steps, then you probably want to focus on pushing the district to take action. If very little exists and there are no clear, logical first steps to take, then you might be better served by building awareness of the needs, and leaving it up to the educators to figure out how to meet those needs.

For example, if all of the classes in your district's middle schools are heterogeneously mixed, and there are no opportunities for differentiation, acceleration, or advanced courses for middle school students, the needs are so broad that there is no clear place to start. Your goal should be to highlight the fact that advanced students are forgotten as a district priority, and to draw contrasts with the approaches used by other (maybe more successful) middle schools in the region or state.

Find Partners and Organize

You won't be able to make this happen as a Lone Ranger. It's too much work, and one individual parent just doesn't have the political clout to change a system. Instead, you need to find partners and organize. Essentially, you want to create a task force that will take responsibility for exploring this topic.

It's key to remember that there is strength in numbers, and that big changes typically only happen when administrators (principals, directors, and/or superintendents) are willing to support them, and when local bigwigs (especially members of the school committee/board) get behind them. If you can, you want to get someone of influence—a principal, a school committee/board member—to sign off on your group to give it legitimacy. (Important note: Some schools have formal parent groups that work with the principal on school policy. If a group like this exists at your school, connect with them, and see if you can attend a meeting and speak to them about your topic.)

Collect Broad and Compelling Data
When it comes to putting new practices or programs in place, everything is pie-in-the-sky until you have some real numbers. You want to know who is interested in the topic, how many students might be impacted, and what the potential fiscal impact might be. Critics will be quick to make counter-arguments—that would cost too much, not many kids would benefit, we have other priorities in the school, training costs would be astronomical, the teachers wouldn't want to do it—and you need to have data to respond and convince.

In addition, you also want to have comparative and "best practice" data. Comparative data looks at how your schools or school system compare to other schools and school systems. If 8 of the 10 nearby school systems that you think of as similar to your system all have formalized "gifted" programs, and your system doesn't, that's important information to share. If the advanced students in your district score below the average of advanced students statewide on standardized tests, that's important information to share (and information that you should be able to find with some digging online, or by teaming up with an ally within the school system). Essentially, anything that shows that your advanced kids aren't provided the same resources, or aren't achieving at the same level, as students in other districts will help to strengthen your case.

Now, you want to be careful to paint an accurate picture and not cherry-pick data that support your argument. If you do start cherry-picking, someone will likely figure that out, and it will ultimately undermine your position. You also don't want to hedge your whole argument on a keeping-up-with-the-Jones' foundation. Ultimately, your goal isn't to try to be better than other districts' kids, but to maximize the educational opportunities for your own kids.

In addition to comparative information, you should identify recognized "best practices." These are practices that are recognized at the state or national level as the sorts of things that high-quality districts do. There are national organizations that advocate for advanced students, such as The National Association for Gifted Children or the National Society for the Gifted and Talented, and they will have a wealth of recommendations on what the best schools and districts do for advanced students. The state may also have recommended guidelines or practices for advanced kids, which should be available on the state's website, or there may be a state gifted organization. Ultimately, you want to be able to inform and support your argument by saying "Here is what the state and national experts say we should be doing."

Present Your Actions and Information Publicly

At the end of the day, public schools should reflect the values and priorities of the communities they serve. In order to advocate for an increased focus on the needs of advanced students, you want to show that there is a sense in the community that this *is* a priority. That means you have to let the community know about what you're doing.

Local newspapers are a great place to get the word out. They are frequently looking for stories to highlight; find out who the reporter is on the local education beat, and see if she is interested in doing a story on your efforts. Local cable access stations can be another option, or local reporters for major TV networks.

One thing you want to be careful about is not casting the district in a negative light, or creating an adversarial relationship. Make sure to highlight any collaborative steps that the district is taking with you and your partners, and try to paint your efforts as working to support the district.

Information nights are also a great way to spread the word. If local principals are on board, see if they would be willing to host an information night at their school, giving you the opportunity to present information to interested parents. Or, even better, see if you can piggy-back off an existing, popular school function and provide flyers or a brief presentation (such as a back-to-school night or holiday concert).

At the conclusion of your work, you want to present a formal report and/or set of recommendations to your district's school committee/board. This then becomes a public document that can be disseminated and discussed. When you do present, make sure you get a large group of people to show up in favor of your report to demonstrate the broad base of support behind your proposal. Especially if your recommendations involve significant financing or school-level action, you want to demonstrate that your proposal reflects the values and priorities of the community.

Notes

1. The website developingchild.harvard.edu is a good resource for more information on this topic.

About the Author

Parry Graham is the assistant superintendent of Wayland Public Schools in Wayland, Massachusetts. He began his career in public education in 1994 as a high school teacher and has spent the last seventeen years in leadership roles at the elementary school, middle school, high school, and central office levels. He is the author of *How Public Schools Really Work: An Insider's Guide for Parents and Practitioners* with Rowman & Littlefield, and coauthor of the books *Making Teamwork Meaningful: Leading Progress-Driven Collaboration in a PLC at Work* and *Building a Professional Learning Community at Work: A Guide to the First Year*. Parry completed his doctorate at UNC-Chapel Hill, where he also worked part-time as a clinical assistant professor in the School of Education.